ST/ESA/STAT/SER.F/95

United Nations Development Group

Led by

United Nations Population Fund

United Nations Development Programme

Department of Economic and
Social Affairs–Statistics Division

D1560434

Indicators for Monitoring the Millennium Development Goals

Definitions | Rationale | Concepts | and Sources

United Nations

New York

2003

NOTE

The designations employed and the presentation of material in this publication do not imply the expression of any opinion whatsoever on the part of the United Nations concerning the legal status of any country, territory, city or area or of its authorities, or concerning the delimitation of its frontiers or boundaries. The term "country" as used in the text of this report refers, as appropriate, to territories or areas. The designations of "developed". "developing" and "least developed" countries are intended for convenience and do not necessarily express a judgement about the stage reached by a particular country or area in the development process. Reference to "dollars" ($) indicates United States dollars, unless otherwise stated.

ST/ESA/STAT/SER.F/95
United Nations Publication
Sales No. E.03.XVII. 18
ISBN 92-1-161467-8
Copyright © United Nations 2003
All rights reserved

Graphic design and Desktop composition Andy Musilli

FOREWORD

Building on the United Nations global conferences of the 1990s, the United Nations Millennium Declaration of 2000 marked a strong commitment to the right to development, to peace and security, to gender equality, to the eradication of the many dimensions of poverty and to sustainable human development. Embedded in that Declaration, which was adopted by 147 heads of State and 189 states, were what have become known as the eight Millennium Development Goals, including 18 time-bound targets.

To monitor progress towards the goals and targets, the United Nations system, including the World Bank and the International Monetary Fund, as well as the Development Assistance Committee of the Organisation for Economic Co-operation and Development, came together under the Office of the Secretary-General and agreed on 48 quantitative indicators. The indicators built upon an intergovernmental process to identify relevant indicators in response to global conferences. The Secretary-General presented the goals, targets and indicators to the General Assembly in September 2001 in his report entitled "Road map towards the implementation of the United Nations Millennium Declaration".

The present handbook provides guidance on the definitions, rationale, concepts and sources of data for each of the indicators that are being used to monitor the goals and targets. It expands on an earlier exercise to provide the metadata for the socio-economic indicators that make up the United Nations Common Country Assessment Indicator Framework. The indicators for goals 1–7 are a subset of that framework.

Preparation of the handbook was directed by an inter-agency working group of the United Nations Development Group, including the World Bank, chaired by the United Nations Population Fund and co-chaired by the United Nations Statistics Division and the United Nations Development Programme. On behalf of the United Nations Development Group, I would like to thank all the agencies and individuals (see below) who contributed to this handbook, including the Department for International Development of the Government of the United Kingdom, which funded the services of a short-term consultant who contributed to the handbook.

I believe that this tangible example of interagency collaboration will prove useful to the international community by strengthening national statistical capacity and improving monitoring. And I sincerely hope that this will be sustained through future revisions in the same spirit.

Mark Malloch Brown
Chairman
United Nations Development Group

September 2003

CONTENTS

ABBREVIATIONS

A, C, E, F, R, S	Translated publications available in Arabic, Chinese, English, French, Russian and Spanish, at http://unstats.un.org.unsd/pubs/
CCA	common country assessment
CFCS	chlorofluorocarbons
c.i.f.	cost, insurance and freight
CWIQ	Core Welfare Indicators Questionnaire in Africa
DAC	Development Assistance Committee of the OECD
DHS	Demographic and Health Survey
DOTS	internationally recommended tuberculosis control strategy
DPT	diphtheria, pertussis and tetanus vaccine
EPI	Expanded Programme on Immunization
FAO	Food and Agriculture Organization of the United Nations
f.o.b.	free on board
GDP	gross domestic product
GNI	gross national income
GNP	gross national product
HBS	household budget survey
HIPC	Heavily Indebted Poor Countries Initiative
ICES	income, consumption and expenditure survey
ILO	Internatonal Labour Organization
IMF	International Monetary Fund
IPU	Inter-Parliamentary Union
ISCED 97	International Standard Classification of Education, 1997 version
ISIC	International Standard Industrial Classification of All Economic Activities
ITU	International Telecommunication Union
IUCN	International Union for Conservation of Nature and Natural Resources–The World Conservation Union
Kg	kilogram
LDCs	least developed countries
LFS	labour force surveys
LSMS	Living Standards Measurement Study
MICS	Multiple Indicator Cluster Survey
NCHS	National Center for Health Statistics
ODA	official development assistance
ODP	ozone-depleting potential
OECD	Organisation for Economic Co-operation and Development
PCs	personal computers
PPP	purchasing power parity
TCBDB	trade capacity-building database
TRAINS	Trade Analysis and Information System
UN-HABITAT	United Nations Human Settlements Programme
UNAIDS	Joint United Nations Programme on HIV/AIDS
UNDP	United Nations Development Programme
UNESCO	United Nations Educational, Scientific and Cultural Organization
UNFPA	United Nations Population Fund
UNICEF	United Nations Children's Fund
WHO	World Health Organization

MEMBERS AND CONTRIBUTORS TO THE UNITED NATIONS DEVELOPMENT GROUP WORKING GROUP ON INDICATORS

United Nations Population Fund
Richard Leete, Chair
Iqbal Alam
Kourtoum Nacro
Mickie Schoch

Department of Economic and Social Affairs Statistics Division
Stefan Schweinfest, Vice Chair
Robert Johnston
Giselle Kamanou
Francesca Perucci

United Nations Development Programme
Diana Alarcon, Vice Chair
Jan Vandemoortele
Haishan Fu

United Nations Development Group Office
Gerton van den Akker
Alain Nickels
Heidi Swindells
Tom Griffin (consultant)

Executive Office of the Secretary-General
Madhushree Dasgupta

United Nations Office on Drugs and Crime
Andrea Treso

Office of the United Nations High Commissioner for Human Rights
Goro Onojima

Joint United Nations Programme on HIV/AIDS
Peter Ghys

United Nations Children's Fund
Gareth Jones
Tessa Wardlaw

United Nations Development Fund for Women
Suzette Mitchell

United Nations Environment Programme
Stuart Chape
Marion Cheatle
Volodymyr Demkine
Eugene Fosnight
Phillip Fox
Gerald Mutisya

United Nations Human Settlements Programme
Laura Licchi

World Food Programme
Patricia Kennedy

Food and Agriculture Organization of the United Nations
Jorge Mernies
Toshiko Murata

International Labour Organization
Sophia Lawrence

International Telecommunication Union
Esperanza Magpantay

United Nations Educational, Scientific and Cultural Organization
Denise Lievesley
José Pessoa

World Bank
Neil Fantom
Makiko Harrison
Eric Swanson

World Health Organization
Christopher Murray
Carla AbouZahr

World Trade Organization
Guy Karsenty

United Nations Framework Convention on Climate Change
James Grabert

Inter-Parliamentary Union
Kareen Jabre

Organisation for Economic Co-operation and Development
Brian Hammond
Simon Scott

INTRODUCTION

Indicators for Monitoring the Millennium Development Goals: Definitions, Rationale, Concepts and Sources contains basic metadata on the agreed list of quantitative indicators for monitoring progress towards the eight goals and 18 targets derived from the United Nations Millennium Declaration (table). The list of indicators, developed using several criteria, is not intended to be prescriptive but to take into account the country setting and the views of various stakeholders in preparing country-level reports.

Five main criteria guided the selection of indicators. Indicators should:
- Provide relevant and robust measures of progress towards the targets of the Millennium Development Goals
- Be clear and straightforward to interpret and provide a basis for international comparison
- Be broadly consistent with other global lists and avoid imposing an unnecessary burden on country teams, Governments and other partners
- Be based to the greatest extent possible on international standards, recommendations and best practices
- Be constructed from well-established data sources, be quantifiable and be consistent to enable measurement over time

The present handbook is designed to provide United Nations country teams and national and international stakeholders with guidance on the definitions, rationale, concepts and sources of the data for the indicators that are being used to monitor the Millennium Development Goals. Just as the indicator list is dynamic and will necessarily evolve in response to changing national situations, so will the metadata change over time as concepts, definitions and methodologies change.

A consultation process, generally involving the national statistical office or other national authority, should be initiated in the selection and compilation of country-specific indicators. The consultation should take into account national development priorities, the suggested list of indicators and the availability of data. The United Nations country team should work collaboratively to help build ownership and consensus on the selected indicators.

NATIONAL SOURCES
Country data should be used for compiling the indicators where such data are available and of reasonable quality. The data source for each indicator and the quantitative value of the indicator should be decided by consensus among the key stakeholders, especially the national statistical system. The national statistical system should own the data and related indicators.

For any given indicator, a wide range of data sources may be available within the country, and each source should be critically reviewed. Existing data sources and reporting systems should be used where possible, particularly where line ministries have their own statistical systems. International data sources should be consulted for validation and in the absence of national sources.

METADATA SHEETS

For each indicator used to measure progress towards the targets and goals, the handbook provides all or some of the following information:

- A simple operational definition
- The goal and target it addresses
- The rationale for use of the indicator
- The method of computation
- Sources of data
- References, including relevant international Web sites
- Periodicity of measurement
- Gender and disaggregation issues
- Limitations of the indicator
- National and international agencies involved in the collection, compilation or dissemination of the data

The intention is not to provide an exhaustive amount of information for each item, but to provide a reference point and guidance for country teams and national stake-holders. The amount of information varies by indicator and tends to reflect the extent of national and international debate on its relevance. Limited information is available for some of the less well-established indicators. With further use of the indicators and greater recognition of the need for such data, fuller information is expected to become available.

Monitoring of the Millennium Development Goals is taking place globally, through annual reports of the United Nations Secretary-General to the General Assembly and through periodic country reporting. For global reporting, use is made of indicators compiled by international organizations. Internationally compiled indicators, based on standard concepts, definitions and methodologies, more readily facilitate cross-country comparisons. For country reporting, use is generally made of indicators compiled from national sources, generally by the national statistical system. The metadata sheets for the indicators reflect national and international standards.

ANNEX 1 provides metadata for some additional indicators included in the common country assessment indicator framework; the indicators for Millennium Development Goals 1–7 are a subset of that framework. ANNEX 2 supplies information on the household surveys and national sources mentioned in the metadata for constructing the indicators. ANNEX 3 gives the World Wide Web addresses of the agencies involved. ANNEX 4 lists the major world summits and conferences that have helped to shape the Millennium Development Goals and indicators.

Goals, targets and indicators

GOALS AND TARGETS FROM THE MILLENNIUM DECLARATION	INDICATORS FOR MONITORING PROGRESS
GOAL 1: ERADICATE EXTREME POVERTY AND HUNGER	
TARGET 1: Halve, between 1990 and 2015, the proportion of people whose income is less than one dollar a day	1. Proportion of population below $1 (PPP) per day[a] 1A. Poverty headcount ratio (percentage of population below the national poverty line) 2. Poverty gap ratio [incidence x depth of poverty] 3. Share of poorest quintile in national consumption
TARGET 2: Halve, between 1990 and 2015, the proportion of people who suffer from hunger	4. Prevalence of underweight children under 5 years of age 5. Proportion of population below minimum level of dietary energy consumption
GOAL 2: ACHIEVE UNIVERSAL PRIMARY EDUCATION	
TARGET 3: Ensure that, by 2015, children everywhere, boys and girls alike, will be able to complete a full course of primary schooling	6. Net enrolment ratio in primary education 7. Proportion of pupils starting grade 1 who reach grade 5[b] 8. Literacy rate of 15–24 year-olds
GOAL 3: PROMOTE GENDER EQUALITY AND EMPOWER WOMEN	
TARGET 4: Eliminate gender disparity in primary and secondary education, preferably by 2005, and in all levels of education no later than 2015	9. Ratio of girls to boys in primary, secondary and tertiary education 10. Ratio of literate women to men, 15–24 years old 11. Share of women in wage employment in the non-agricultural sector 12. Proportion of seats held by women in national parliament
GOAL 4: REDUCE CHILD MORTALITY	
TARGET 5: Reduce by two thirds, between 1990 and 2015, the under-five mortality rate	13. Under-five mortality rate 14. Infant mortality rate 15. Proportion of 1 year-old children immunized against measles
GOAL 5: IMPROVE MATERNAL HEALTH	
TARGET 6: Reduce by three quarters, between 1990 and 2015, the maternal mortality ratio	16. Maternal mortality ratio 17. Proportion of births attended by skilled health personnel
GOAL 6: COMBAT HIV/AIDS, MALARIA AND OTHER DISEASES	
TARGET 7: Have halted by 2015 and begun to reverse the spread of HIV/AIDS	18. HIV prevalence among pregnant women aged 15–24 years 19. Condom use rate of the contraceptive prevalence rate[c] 19A. Condom use at last high-risk sex 19B. Percentage of population aged 15-24 years with comprehensive correct knowledge of HIV/AIDS[d] 19C. Contraceptive prevalence rate 20. Ratio of school attendance of orphans to school attendance of non-orphans aged 10–14years
TARGET 8: Have halted by 2015 and begun to reverse the incidence of malaria and other major diseases	21. Prevalence and death rates associated with malaria 22. Proportion of population in malaria-risk areas using effective malaria prevention and treatment measures[e] 23. Prevalence and death rates associated with tuberculosis 24. Proportion of tuberculosis cases detected and cured under DOTS
GOAL 7: ENSURE ENVIRONMENTAL SUSTAINABILITY	
TARGET 9: Integrate the principles of sustainable development into country policies and programmes and reverse the loss of environmental resources	25. Proportion of land area covered by forest 26. Ratio of area protected to maintain biological diversity to surface area 27. Energy use (kg oil equivalent) per $1 GDP (PPP) 28. Carbon dioxide emissions per capita and consumption of ozone-depleting CFCs (ODP tons) 29. Proportion of population using solid fuels
TARGET 10: Halve, by 2015, the proportion of people without sustainable access to safe drinking water and basic sanitation	30. Proportion of population with sustainable access to an improved water source, urban and rural 31. Proportion of population with access to improved sanitation, urban and rural
TARGET 11: By 2020, to have achieved a significant improvement in the lives of at least 100 million slum dwellers	32. Proportion of households with access to secure tenure

GOAL 8: DEVELOP A GLOBAL PARTNERSHIP FOR DEVELOPMENT	*Some of the indicators listed below are monitored separately for the least developed countries (LDCs), Africa, landlocked countries and small island developing States.*
TARGET 12 : Develop further an open, rule-based, predictable, non-discriminatory trading and financial system Includes a commitment to good governance, development and poverty reduction – both nationally and internationally	**Official development assistance** 33. Net ODA, total and to the least developed countries, as a percentage of OECD/DAC donors' gross national income 34. Proportion of total bilateral, sector-allocable ODA of OECD/DAC donors to basic social services (basic education, primary health care, nutrition, safe water and sanitation)
TARGET 13 : Address the special needs of the least developed countries Includes: tariff and quota free access for the least developed countries' exports; enhanced programme of debt relief for heavily indebted poor countries (HIPC) and cancellation of official bilateral debt; and more generous ODA for countries committed to poverty reduction	35. Proportion of bilateral official development assistance of OECD/DAC donors that is untied 36. ODA received in landlocked countries as a proportion of their gross national incomes 37. ODA received in small island developing States as proportion of their gross national incomes
TARGET 14 : Address the special needs of landlocked countries and small island developing States (through the Programme of Action for the Sustainable Development of Small Island Developing States and the outcome of the twenty-second special session of the General Assembly)	**Market access** 38. Proportion of total developed country imports (by value and excluding arms) from developing countries and and from the least developed countries, admitted free of duty 39. Average tariffs imposed by developed countries on agricultural products and textiles and clothing from developing countries
TARGET 15 : Deal comprehensively with the debt problems of developing countries through national and international measures in order to make debt sustainable in the long term	40. Agricultural support estimate for OECD countries as a percentage of their gross domestic product 41. Proportion of ODA provided to help build trade capacity **Debt sustainability** 42. Total number of countries that have reached their HIPC decision points and number that have reached their HIPC completion points (cumulative) 43. Debt relief committed under HIPC Initiative 44. Debt service as a percentage of exports of goods and services
TARGET 16 : In cooperation with developing countries, develop and implement strategies for decent and productive work for youth	45. Unemployment rate of young people aged 15-24 years, each sex and total[f]
TARGET 17 : In cooperation with pharmaceutical companies, provide access to affordable essential drugs in developing countries	46. Proportion of population with access to affordable essential drugs on a sustainable basis
TARGET 18 : In cooperation with the private sector, make available the benefits of new technologies, especially information and communications	47. Telephone lines and cellular subscribers per 100 population 48A. Personal computers in use per 100 population and Internet users per 100 population 48B. Internet users per 100 population

THE MILLENNIUM DEVELOPMENT GOALS and targets come from the Millennium Declaration, signed by 189 countries, including 147 heads of State and Government, in September 2000 (http://www.un.org.millennium/declaration/ares552e.htm). The goals and targets are interrelated and should be seen as a whole. They represent a partnership between the developed countries and the developing countries "to create an environment – at the national and global levels alike – which is conducive to development and the elimination of poverty".

Note: Goals, targets and indicators effective 8 September 2003.

a For monitoring country poverty trends, indicators based on national poverty lines should be used, where available.

b An alternative indicator under development is "primary completion rate".

c Among contraceptive methods, only condoms are effective in preventing HIV transmission. Since the condom use rate is only measured among women in union, it is supplemented by an indicator on condom use in high-risk situations (indicator 19a) and an indicator on HIV/AIDS knowledge (indicator 19b). Indicator 19c (contraceptive prevalence rate) is also useful in tracking progress in other health, gender and poverty goals.

d This indicator is defined as the percentage of population aged 15-24 who correctly identify the two major ways of preventing the sexual transmission of HIV (using condoms and limiting sex to one faithful, uninfected partner), who reject the two most common local misconceptions about HIV transmission, and who know that a healthy-looking person can transmit HIV. However, since there are currently not a sufficient number of surveys to be able to calculate the indicator as defined above, UNICEF, in collaboration with UNAIDS and WHO, produced two proxy indicators that represent two components of the actual indicator. They are the following: (a) percentage of women and men 15-24 who know that a person can protect herself from HIV infection by "consistent use of condom"; (b) percentage of women and men 15-24 who know a healthy-looking person can transmit HIV.

e Prevention to be measured by the percentage of children under 5 sleeping under insecticide-treated bednets; treatment to be measured by percentage of children under 5 who are appropriately treated.

f An improved measure of the target for future years is under development by the International Labour Organization.

1 PROPORTION OF POPULATION BELOW $1 PURCHASING POWER PARITY(PPP) PER DAY

DEFINITION

Proportion of population below $1 per day is the percentage of the population living on less than $1.08 a day at 1993 international prices. The one dollar a day poverty line is compared to consumption or income per person and includes consumption from own production and income in kind. This poverty line has fixed purchasing power across countries or areas and is often called an "absolute poverty line" or measure of extreme poverty.

GOAL AND TARGET ADDRESSED

Goal 1. Eradicate extreme poverty and hunger
Target 1. Halve, between 1990 and 2015, the proportion of people whose income is less than one dollar a day

RATIONALE

The indicator allows for comparing and aggregating progress across countries in reducing the number of people living under extreme poverty and for monitoring trends at the global level.

METHOD OF COMPUTATION

The World Bank regularly estimates poverty based on the one dollar a day poverty line. Estimates are based on incomes or consumption levels derived from household surveys. Whenever possible, consumption is preferred to income for measuring poverty. When consumption data are not available, income is used.

Consumption, which includes consumption for own production, or income per person, and its distribution are estimated from household surveys. Household consumption or income is divided by the number of people in the household to establish the income per person.

The distribution of consumption or income is estimated using empirical Lorenz (distribu-tion) curves weighted by household size. In all cases measures of poverty to obtain Lorenz curves are calculated from primary data sources rather than existing estimates.

Poverty in a country is estimated by converting the one dollar a day poverty line to local currency using the latest purchasing power parity (PPP) exchange rates for consumption taken from World Bank estimates. Local consumer price indices are then used to adjust the international poverty line in local currency to prices prevailing around the time of the surveys. This international poverty line is used to identify how many people are below the one dollar a day threshold.

The PPP-based international poverty line is required only to allow comparisons across countries and to produce estimates of poverty at the aggregate level. Most countries also set their own poverty lines (SEE INDICATOR 1A).

DATA COLLECTION AND SOURCE

The indicator is produced by the World Bank Development Research Group based on data obtained from government statistical offices and World Bank country departments. It is not normally calculated by national agencies.

Data on household income, consumption and expenditure, including income in kind, are generally collected through household budget surveys or other surveys covering income and expenditure.

When available, household consumption data are preferred to income data. National statistical offices, sometimes in conjunction with other national or international agencies, usually undertake such surveys.

Only surveys that meet the following criteria are used: they are nationally representative, include a sufficiently comprehensive consumption or income aggregate (including consumption or income from own production), and they allow for the construction of a correctly weighted distribution of consumption or income per person.

The most recent estimates of PPP for developing countries are based on data collected between 1993 and 1996, standardized to 1993 international prices. Global price comparisons are carried out by the International Comparison Programme of the World Bank and others. New estimates of PPPs are expected in 2006.

PERIODICITY OF MEASUREMENT

Household budget or income surveys are undertaken at different intervals in different countries. In developing countries they typically take place every three to five years.

PPP surveys are conducted at infrequent intervals. The last price survey through the International Comparison Programme was completed in 1996, and the next will begin in 2003. It is, however, possible to extrapolate from PPP surveys, and the World Bank conversion factors are calculated in this way.

GENDER ISSUES

Households headed by women tend to have lower incomes and are therefore more likely to have incomes per person lower than one dollar. However, this relationship should be carefully studied to take into account national circumstances and the definition of head of household adopted in data collection, which is not necessarily related to being the chief source of economic support. Whether households are headed by women or men, gender relations affect intrahousehold resource allocation and use. It is not possible to estimate sex-disaggregated poverty rates from available data.

DISAGGREGATION ISSUES

It is sometimes possible to disaggregate this indicator by urban-rural location.

COMMENTS AND LIMITATIONS

The one dollar a day poverty measure is used to assess and monitor poverty at the global level, but like other indicators it is not equally relevant in all regions because countries have different definitions of poverty. Measurements of poverty in countries are generally based on national poverty lines.

PPP exchange rates are used because they take into account the local prices of goods and services that are not traded internationally. Although PPP rates were designed for comparing aggregates from national accounts, they may not fully reflect the comparative cost of goods typically consumed by the very poor.

There are also problems in comparing poverty measures within countries, especially for urban-rural differences. The cost of living is typically higher in urban than in rural areas, so the urban monetary poverty line should be higher than the rural monetary poverty line. However, it is not always clear that the difference between the two poverty lines found in practice properly reflects the difference in the cost of living.

In considering whether to use income or consumption as a welfare indicator, income is generally more difficult to measure accurately, and consumption accords better with the idea of the standard of living than income, which can vary over time even if the standard of living does not. Nevertheless, consumption data are not always available, and when they are not there is little choice but to use income.

There is also a problem with comparability across surveys: household survey questionnaires can differ widely, and even similar surveys may not be strictly comparable because of differences in quality.

Even if surveys are entirely accurate, the measure of poverty can miss some important aspects of individual welfare. First, using household consumption ignores inequalities within households. Second, the measure does not reflect people's feeling about relative deprivation or their concerns about uninsured risks to their income and health.

Comparisons across countries at different levels of development may also pose a problem, owing to differences in the relative importance of consumption of non-market goods.

REFERENCES AND INTERNATIONAL DATA COMPARISONS

▶ **CHEN, SHAOCHUA,** and **MARTIN RAVALLION** (2002). *How Did the World's Poorest Fare in the 1990s?*, Working Paper No. 2409, pp.1-5. Washington, D.C.: World Bank. Available from http://www.worldbank.org/research/povmonitor/publications.htm.

▶ **HESTON, ALAN, ROBERT SUMMERS** *and* **BETTINA ATEN** (2002). *Penn World Tables 6.1. Internet site* http://datacentre2.chass.utoronto.ca/pwt .

▶ **UNITED NATIONS** (1992). *Handbook of the International Comparison Programme.* Series F, No. 62 (United Nations publication, Sales No. E.92.XVII.12). Available from http://unstats.un.org/unsd/pubs. (A, C, E, F, R, S)

▶ **UNITED NATIONS** (2003). *Millennium Indicators Database.* Statistics Division Internet site http://millenniumindicators.un.org.

▶ **UNITED NATIONS DEVELOPMENT PROGRAMME** (2003 and annual). *Human Development Report.* New York: Oxford University Press. Available from http://hdr.undp.org.

▶ **UNITED NATIONS, COMMISSION OF THE EUROPEAN COMMUNITIES, INTERNATIONAL MONETARY FUND, ORGANISATION FOR ECONOMIC CO-OPERATION AND DEVELOPMENT AND WORLD BANK** (1994). *System of National Accounts 1993 (SNA 1993)*, Series F, No. 2, Rev. 4 (United Nations publication, Sales No. E.94.XVII.4), paras. 9.45, 16.80-16.83. Available with updates from http://unstats.un.org/unsd/sna1993.

▶ **WORLD BANK** (2001). *Poverty Reduction and the World Bank: Progress in Operationalizing the World Development Report*

2000/01. Washington, D.C. Available from http://www.worldbank.org/poverty/library/progr/2000-01/execsum.htm.

▶ **WORLD BANK** (2003 and annual). *World Development Indicators*. Print and CD-ROM. Table 2.6. Washington, D.C. Available in part from http://www.worldbank.org/data.

▶ **WORLD BANK** (2003). *Data and Statistics*. Internet site http://www.worldbank.org/data . Washington, D.C.

▶ **WORLD BANK** (2003). *Poverty Reduction Strategy Sourcebook*, vol. 1, *Core techniques: Poverty Measurement and Analysis*. Washington, D.C. Available from http://www.worldbank.org/poverty/strategies/sourcons.htm .

AGENCY
World Bank

1.A POVERTY HEADCOUNT RATIO (PERCENTAGE OF POPULATION BELOW THE NATIONAL POVERTY LINE)

DEFINITION
The poverty headcount ratio is the proportion of the national population whose incomes are below the official threshold (or thresholds) set by the national Government. National poverty lines are usually set for households of various compositions to allow for different family sizes. Where there are no official poverty lines, they may be defined as the level of income required to have only sufficient food or food plus other necessities for survival.

GOAL AND TARGET ADDRESSED
Goal 1. Eradicate extreme poverty and hunger
Target 1. Halve, between 1990 and 2015, the proportion of people whose income is less than one dollar a day

RATIONALE
The indicator allows for monitoring the proportion of the national population that is considered poor by a national standard. Most

poverty analysis work for countries is based on national poverty lines. National poverty lines tend to increase in purchasing power with the average level of income of a country.

METHOD OF COMPUTATION
Household income (or consumption) and its distribution are estimated from household surveys (SEE INDICATOR 1). The incomes of various household types, by composition, may then be compared with the poverty lines for those types of household. If the poverty lines are expressed in terms of income per adult equivalent or some similar measure, the incomes of the households must be measured on a similar basis. Household income may be converted to income per adult equivalent by using the modified equivalence scale of the Organisation for Economic Co-operation and Development (OECD)—in which the first household member over 16 equals 1, all others over 16 equal 0.5, all under 16 equal 0.3 —or some other equivalence scale. Household incomes are then divided by the "equivalized" number of people in the household (two adults would equal 1.5 according to the OECD scale) to establish income per person.

Once the number of households that are below the poverty line has been estimated, the number of people in those households is aggregated to estimate the percentage of the population below the line.

DATA COLLECTION AND SOURCE
Data on household income, consumption and expenditure, including income in kind, are generally collected through household budget surveys or other surveys covering income and expenditure.

National statistical offices, sometimes in conjunction with other national or international agencies, usually undertake such surveys.

PERIODICITY OF MEASUREMENT
Household budget or income surveys are undertaken at different intervals in different countries. In developing countries they typically take place every three to five years.

GENDER ISSUES
Households headed by women tend to have lower incomes and are therefore more likely to have incomes per person below the poverty line. However, this relationship should be carefully studied to take into account national circumstances and the definition of head of household adopted in data collection, which is not necessarily related to being the chief source of economic support. Whether households are headed by women or men, gender relations affect intrahousehold resource allocation and use.

DISAGGREGATION ISSUES
Disaggregation of the poverty headcount index is normally limited by the size of the household survey. It is common, however, for indices to be produced for urban and rural areas and for some subnational levels as the sample allows. Estimates at low levels of disaggregation may be made using "poverty mapping" techniques, which use the lower levels of disaggregation available from population censuses, particularly where the timing of the population census and household survey is relatively close. Wherever household surveys provide income or consumption data disaggregated by sex of household heads, these data should be used.

COMMENTS AND LIMITATIONS
The advantage of this indicator is that it is specific to the country in which the data are collected and where the poverty line is established. While the one dollar a day poverty line helps in making international comparisons, national poverty lines are used to make more accurate estimates of poverty consistent with the characteristics and level of development of each country. The disadvantage is that there is no universally agreed poverty line, even in principle, and international comparisons are not feasible.

There are also problems in comparing poverty measures within countries, especially for urban and rural differences. The cost of living is typically higher in urban than in rural areas, so the urban monetary poverty line should be higher than the rural monetary poverty line. But it is not always clear that the difference between the two poverty lines found in practice properly reflects the difference in the cost of living.

REFERENCES AND INTERNATIONAL DATA COMPARISONS

▸ CANBERRA GROUP ON HOUSEHOLD INCOME STATISTICS (2001). *Expert Group on Household Income Statistics: Final Report and Recommendations*. Ottawa. Available from http://www.lisproject.org/links/canb access.htm.

▸ SWEDEN, STATISTICS SWEDEN (1996). *Engendering Statistics: A Tool for Change*. Stockholm.

▸ UNITED NATIONS (2003). *Millennium Indicators Database*. Statistics Division Internet site http://millenniumindicators.un.org.

▸ UNITED NATIONS DEVELOPMENT PROGRAMME (2003 and annual). *Human Development Report*. New York, Oxford University Press. Available from http://hdr.undp.org.

▸ WORLD BANK (2003 and annual). *World Development Indicators*. Print and CD-ROM. Notes to table 2.6. Washington, D.C. Available in part from http://www.world bank.org/data.

▸ WORLD BANK (2003). *Poverty Reduction Strategy Sourcebook*, vol. 1, *Core Techniques: Poverty Measurement and Analysis*. Washington, D.C. Available from http://www.worldbank.org/poverty/strategies/sourcons.htm.

AGENCIES

National statistical offices
World Bank

2 POVERTY GAP RATIO (INCIDENCE MULTIPLIED BY DEPTH OF POVERTY)

DEFINITION

Poverty gap ratio is the mean distance separating the population from the poverty line (with the non-poor being given a distance of zero), expressed as a percentage of the poverty line.

GOAL AND TARGET ADDRESSED

Goal 1. Eradicate extreme poverty and hunger
Target 1. Halve, between 1990 and 2015, the proportion of people whose income is less than one dollar a day

RATIONALE

The indicator measures the "poverty deficit" of the entire population, where the poverty deficit is the per capita amount of resources that would be needed to bring all poor people above the poverty line through perfectly targeted cash transfers.

METHOD OF COMPUTATION

The poverty gap ratio is the sum of the income gap ratios for the population below the poverty line, divided by the total population, which can be expressed as follows:

$$PG = \frac{1}{n}\sum_{i=1}^{q}\left[\frac{z - Y_i}{z}\right]$$

where z is the poverty line, Y_i is the income of individual i, q is the number of poor people and n is the size of the population. The poverty gap can also be expressed (and thus calculated) as the product of the average income gap ratio of poor people and the headcount ratio, that is,

where

$$PG = I * H$$

where

$$H = \frac{q}{n} \quad I = \frac{z - Y_q}{z}$$

where

$$Y_q = \frac{1}{q}\sum_{i=1}^{q} Y_i$$

All the formulas are calculated based on data on individuals (Y_i as individual income or consumption). If household-level data are used, the formulas have to be adjusted by the weight w_i, which is the household size times sampling expansion factor for every household i.

DATA COLLECTION AND SOURCE

When based on the $1 a day poverty line, this indicator is calculated by the World Bank. When based on national poverty lines, the indicator is commonly calculated by national agencies.

The data required are the same as those for indicator 1.

PERIODICITY OF MEASUREMENT

Household budget or income surveys are undertaken at different intervals in different countries. In developing countries, they typically take place every three to five years.

GENDER ISSUES

Households headed by women may be concentrated in the bottom fifth. However, this relationship should be carefully studied to take into account national circumstances and the definition of head of household adopted in data collection, which is not necessarily related to being the chief source of economic support. Whether households are headed by women or men, gender relations affect intra-household resource allocation and use.

COMMENTS AND LIMITATIONS

The comments under indicators 1 and 1A also apply here.

This measure can also be used for non-monetary indicators, provided that the measure of the distance is meaningful. For example, the poverty gap in education could be the number of years of education missing to reach the defined threshold.

REFERENCES AND INTERNATIONAL DATA COMPARISONS

▸ CHEN, SHAOCHUA, and MARTIN RAVALLION (2002). *How Did the World's Poorest Fare in the 1990s?* Working Paper No. 2409, pp.1-5. World Bank, Washington, D.C. Available from http://www.worldbank.org/research/povmonitor/publications.htm .
▸ UNITED NATIONS (2003). *Millennium Indicators Database*. Statistics Division Internet site http://millenniumindicators.un.org .
▸ WORLD BANK (2003 and annual). *World Development Indicators*. Print and CD-ROM. Washington, D.C. Available in part from http://www.worldbank.org/data .
▸ WORLD BANK (2003). *Poverty Reduction Strategy Sourcebook, vol. 1, Core Techniques: Poverty Measurement and Analysis*. Washington, D.C. Available from http://www.worldbank.org/poverty/strategies/sourcons.htm.

AGENCIES
National statistical offices
World Bank

3 SHARE OF POOREST QUINTILE IN NATIONAL CONSUMPTION

DEFINITION
Share of the poorest quintile in national consumption is the income that accrues to the poorest fifth of the population.

GOAL AND TARGET ADDRESSED
Goal 1. Eradicate extreme poverty and hunger
Target 1. Halve, between 1990 and 2015, the proportion of people whose income is less than one dollar a day

RATIONALE

The indicator provides information about the distribution of consumption or income of the poorest fifth of the population. Because the consumption of the poorest fifth is expressed as a percentage of total household consumption (or income), this indicator is a "relative inequality" measure. Therefore, while the absolute consumption of the poorest fifth may increase, its share of total consumption may remain the same (if the total goes up by the same proportion), decline (if the total goes up by a larger proportion) or increase (if the total goes up by a smaller proportion).

METHOD OF COMPUTATION

Household income and its distribution are estimated from household surveys. Household income is adjusted for household size to provide a more consistent measure of per capita income for consumption. Household income is divided by the number of people in the household to establish income per person. The population is then ranked by income. The income of the bottom fifth is expressed as a percentage of aggregate household income. The calculations are made in local currency, without adjustment for price changes or exchange rates or for spatial differences in cost of living within countries, because the data needed for such calculations are generally unavailable.

DATA COLLECTION AND SOURCE

For international purposes, this indicator is calculated by the World Bank, but it may also be calculated by national agencies. The Development Research Group of the World Bank Group produces the indicator based on primary household survey data obtained from government statistical agencies and World Bank country departments.

Data on household income or consumption come from household surveys. Since underlying household surveys differ across countries in methods and type of data collected, the World Bank tries to produce comparable data for international comparisons and for analysis at the aggregated level (regional or global). Survey data provide either per capita income or consumption. Whenever possible, consumption data are used rather than income data. Where the original household survey data are not available, shares are estimated from the best available grouped data.

PERIODICITY OF MEASUREMENT

Household budget or income surveys are undertaken at different intervals in different countries. In developing countries, they typically take place every three to five years.

GENDER ISSUES

Households headed by women may be concentrated in the bottom fifth. However, this relationship should be carefully studied to take into account national circumstances and the definition of head of household adopted in data collection, which is not necessarily related to the chief source of economic support. Whether households are headed by women or men, gender relations affect intra-household resource allocation and use.

INTERNATIONAL DATA COMPARISONS

Since the underlying household surveys differ in method and type of data collected, the distribution indicators are not easily comparable across countries. These problems are diminishing as survey methods improve and become more standardized, but achieving strict comparability is still impossible (see "COMMENTS AND LIMITATIONS" for INDICATOR 1).

COMMENTS AND LIMITATIONS

Two sources of non-comparability should be noted. First, the surveys can differ in many respects, including whether they use income or consumption as the indicator of living standards. The distribution of income is typically more unequal than the distribution of consumption. In addition, the definitions of income usually differ among surveys. Consumption is normally a better welfare indicator, particularly in developing countries (see "COMMENTS AND LIMITATIONS" for INDICATOR 1).

Second, households differ in size (number of members), extent of income sharing among members, age of members and consumption needs. Differences among countries in these respects may bias comparisons of distribution.

The percentile chosen here is the bottom fifth (quintile). The proportionate share of national household income of this group may go up while the proportionate share of some other percentile, such as the bottom tenth (decile), may go down, and vice versa.

REFERENCES AND INTERNATIONAL DATA COMPARISONS

▶ RAVALLION, MARTIN, and SHAOHUA CHEN (1996). What Can New Survey Data Tell Us about Recent Change in Distribution and Poverty? *World Bank Economic Review*. Washington, D.C. 11/2:357-82.
▶ UNITED NATIONS (2001). *Indicators of Sustainable Development: Guidelines and Methodologies*. Department of Economic and Social Affairs, Division for Sustainable Development. Sales No. E.01.II.A.6. Available from http:// www.un.org/esa/ sustdev/natlinfo/indicators/isd.htm .
▶ UNITED NATIONS (2003). *Millennium Indicators Database*. Statistics Division Internet site http://millenniumindicators.un.org .
▶ WORLD BANK (2003 and annual). *World Development Indicators*. Print and CD-ROM. Washington, D.C. Available in part from http://www.worldbank.org/data .

AGENCIES
National statistical offices
World Bank

4 PREVALENCE OF UNDERWEIGHT CHILDREN UNDER 5 YEARS OF AGE

DEFINITION
Prevalence of (moderately or severely) *underweight children* is the percentage of children under five years old whose weight for age is less than minus two standard deviations from the median for the international reference population ages 0–59 months. The international reference population was formulated by the National Center for Health Statistics (NCHS) as a reference for the United States and later adopted by the World Health Organization (WHO) for international use (often referred to as the NCHS/WHO reference population).

GOAL AND TARGET ADDRESSED
Goal 1. Eradicate extreme poverty and hunger
Target 2. Halve, between 1990 and 2015, the proportion of people who suffer from hunger

RATIONALE
Child malnutrition, as reflected in body weight, is selected as an indicator for several reasons. Child malnutrition is linked to poverty, low levels of education and poor access to health services. Malnourishment in children, even moderate, increases their risk of death, inhibits their cognitive development, and affects health status later in life. Sufficient and good quality nutrition is the cornerstone for development, health and survival of current and succeeding generations. Healthy nutrition is particularly important for women during pregnancy and lactation so that their children set off on sound developmental paths, both physically and mentally. Only when optimal child growth is ensured for the majority of their people will Governments be successful in their efforts to accelerate economic development in a sustained way.

The under-five underweight prevalence is an internationally recognized public health indicator for monitoring nutritional status and health in populations. Child malnutrition is also monitored more closely than adult malnutrition.

METHOD OF COMPUTATION
The weights of the under-five child population in a country are compared with the weights given in the NCHS/WHO table of child weights for each age group. The percentages of children in each age group whose weights are more than 2 standard deviations less than the median are then aggregated to form the total percentage of children under age 5 who are underweight.

DATA COLLECTION AND SOURCE
At the national level, data are generally available from national household surveys, including Demographic and Health Surveys, Multiple Indicator Cluster Surveys and national nutrition surveys.

For international comparisons and global or regional monitoring, the United Nations Children's Fund (UNICEF) and WHO compile international data series and estimate regional and global figures based on data from national surveys.

PERIODICITY OF MEASUREMENT
Household surveys are generally conducted every three to five years.

GENDER ISSUES
The data from national household surveys generally show no significant differences in underweight prevalence between boys and girls. However, those trends should continue to be monitored, particularly at the subnational level and within subgroups of the population.

DISAGGREGATION ISSUES
Indicators of malnutrition generally show differentials between rural and urban settings. In some countries, child nutrition may vary across geographical areas, socio-economic groups or ethnic groups. However, showing and analysing data on specific ethnic groups

may be a sensitive issue in the country. Gender differences may also be more pronounced in some social and ethnic groups.

COMMENTS AND LIMITATIONS
The weight-for-age indicator reflects body mass relative to chronological age and is influenced by both the height of the child (height for age) and weight-for-height. Its composite nature makes interpretation complex. For example, weight for age fails to distinguish between short children of adequate body weight and tall, thin children.

Low height for age or stunting, defined as minus two standard deviations from the median height for the age of the reference population, measures the cumulative deficient growth asociated with long-term factors, including chronic insufficient daily protein intake.

Low weight for height, or wasting, defined as below minus 2 standard deviations from the median weight for height of the reference population, indicates in most cases a recent and severe process of weight loss, often associated with acute starvation or severe disease.

When possible, all three indicators should be analysed and presented since they measure and reflect different aspects of child malnutrition.

REFERENCES AND INTERNATIONAL DATA COMPARISONS
▸ UNITED NATIONS CHILDREN'S FUND (2003). *Progress since the World Summit for Children*. New York. Available from http://www.childinfo.org.
▸ UNITED NATIONS CHILDREN'S FUND (annual). *The State of the World's Children*. New York.
▸ UNITED NATIONS (2001). *Indicators of Sustainable Development: Guidelines and Methodologies*. Department of Economic and Social Affairs, Division for Sustainable Development. Sales No. E.01.II.A. Available from http:// www.un.org/esa/sustdev/natlinfo/indicitors/isd.htm.
▸ UNITED NATIONS (2003). *Millennium Indicators*

Database. Statistics Division Internet site http://millenniumindicators.un.org .

▶ WORLD BANK (2003 and annual). *World Development Indicators*. Print and CD-ROM. Washington, D.C. Available in part from http://www.worldbank.org/data .

▶ WORLD HEALTH ORGANIZATION (1986). *The Growth Chart: A Tool for Use in Infant and Child Health Care*. Geneva.

▶ WORLD HEALTH ORGANIZATION (2002 and annual). *World Health Report*. Geneva. Available from http://www.who.int/whr/en.

▶ WORLD HEALTH ORGANIZATION (2003). *Global Database on Child Growth and Malnutrition*. Internet site http://www.who.int/nut-growthdb/. Geneva.

UNICEF and WHO produce international data sets based on survey data. In some countries, ages may have to be estimated.

AGENCIES
Ministries of health
United Nations Children's Fund
World Health Organization

5 PROPORTION OF THE POPULATION BELOW MINIMUM LEVEL OF DIETARY ENERGY CONSUMPTION

DEFINITION
Proportion of the population below the minimum level of dietary energy consumption is the percentage of the population whose food intake falls below the minimum level of dietary energy requirements. This is also referred to as the prevalence of under-nourishment, which is the percentage of the population that is undernourished.

GOAL AND TARGET ADDRESSED
Goal 1. Eradicate extreme poverty and hunger
Target 2. Halve, between 1990 and 2015, the proportion of people who suffer from hunger

RATIONALE
The indicator measures an important aspect of the food insecurity of a population. Sustainable development demands a concerted effort to reduce poverty, including finding solutions to hunger and malnutrition. Alleviating hunger is a prerequisite for sustainable poverty reduction since undernourishment seriously affects labour productivity and earning capacity. Malnutrition can be the outcome of a range of circumstances. In order to work, poverty reduction strategies must address food access, availability (physical and economic) and safety.

METHOD OF COMPUTATION
Estimation of the proportion of people with insufficient food (undernourishment) involves specification of the distribution of dietary energy consumption, considering the total food availability (from national global statistics) and inequality in access to food (from national household surveys). The distribution is assumed to be unimodal and skewed. The log-normal function is used in estimating the proportion of the population below a minimum energy requirement level or cut-off point. The cut-off point is estimated as a population per capita average value, based on dietary energy needed by different age and gender groups and the proportion of the population represented by each age group.

The estimates are not normally available in countries. The Food and Agriculture Organization of the United Nations (FAO) prepares the estimates at the national level. They are then aggregated to obtain regional and global estimates.

DATA COLLECTION AND SOURCE
The main data sources are country statistics on local food production, trade, stocks and non-food uses; food consumption data from national household surveys; country anthropometric data by sex and age and United Nations country population estimates, in total and by sex and age.

PERIODICITY OF MEASUREMENT

Estimates for the most recent period and for selected benchmark periods (expressed as three-year averages) are reported every year.

GENDER ISSUES

Intrahousehold access to food may show disparities by gender. Also, cultural patterns of distribution and nutritional taboos may affect women's nutrition. Women's higher requirements for iron during pregnancy and breastfeeding may result in iron deficiency anemia, which affects the result of pregnancy and may increase women's susceptibility to diseases. Although food consumption data do not allow for disaggregation by sex, whenever household survey data are available by sex, efforts should be made to conduct a gender-based analysis.

DISAGGREGATION ISSUES

In assessing food insecurity, it is important to consider geographical areas that may be particularly vulnerable (such as areas with a high probability of major variations in production or supply or areas subject to natural disasters) and the population groups whose access to food is precarious or sporadic (due to structural or economic vulnerability), such as ethnic or social groups. However, showing and analysing data on specific ethnic groups may be a sensitive issue in the country. Gender differences may also be more pronounced in some social and ethnic groups.

Considering the need for disaggregated estimates, the FAO methodology has been expanded to measure the extent of food deprivation at subnational levels, making appropriate use of available household survey data. To support countries in preparing disaggregated estimates, FAO is conducting capacity-building activities for national statistical offices.

COMMENTS AND LIMITATIONS

The methods and data used by FAO have implications for the precise meaning and significance of resulting estimates for assessment and policy-making. First, the estimates are based on food acquired by (or available to) the households rather than the actual food intake of individual household members. Second, any inequity in intrahousehold access to food is not taken into account. Third, changes in relative inequality of food distribution through the assessed periods are not considered. However, FAO is monitoring any evidence of significant changes over time that would require adjustment to the current estimation procedure.

Indicators should not be used in isolation. Monitoring of the hunger reduction target addresses two related problems: food deprivation and child malnutrition. Analysis of food deprivation is based on estimates of the prevalence of undernourishment in the whole population. Analysis of child malnutrition is based on estimates of underweight prevalence in the child population. This is an indicator of nutritional status of individual children (adequate weight for a given age), and the final outcome depends not only on food adequacy but also on other multiple factors such as infections, environmental conditions and care. Therefore, the combined use of both indicators would enhance the understanding of the changes in the food and nutrition situation.

REFERENCES AND INTERNATIONAL DATA COMPARISONS

▶ FOOD AND AGRICULTURE ORGANIZATION OF THE UNITED NATIONS (2002). FAO Methodology for Estimating the Prevalence of Undernourishment. In *Proceedings of the International Scientific Symposium on Measurement and Assessment of Food Deprivation and Undernutrition*. Rome.

▶ FOOD AND AGRICULTURE ORGANIZATION OF THE UNITED NATIONS (annual). *The State of Food Insecurity in the World*. Rome. Available from http://www.fao.org/sof/sofi/index_en. htm .

▶ WORLD HEALTH ORGANIZATION (1985). *Energy*

and Protein Requirements: Report of a Joint FAO/WHO/UNU Expert Consultation.* World Health Organization Technical Report 724. Geneva.

AGENCY

Food and Agriculture Organization of the United Nations

6 NET ENROLMENT RATIO IN PRIMARY EDUCATION

DEFINITION

Net primary enrolment ratio is the ratio of the number of children of official school age (as defined by the national education system) who are enrolled in primary school to the total population of children of official school age. *Primary education* provides children with basic reading, writing, and mathematics skills along with an elementary understanding of such subjects as history, geography, natural science, social science, art and music

GOAL AND TARGET ADDRESSED

Goal 2. Achieve universal primary education
Target 3. Ensure that, by 2015, children everywhere, boys and girls alike, will be able to complete a full course of primary schooling

RATIONALE

The indicator is used to monitor progress towards the goal of achieving universal primary education, identified in both the Millennium Development Goals and the Education for All initiative. It shows the proportion of children of primary school age who are enrolled in primary school. Net enrolment refers only to children of official primary school age. (Gross enrolment includes children of any age.) Net enrolment rates below 100 per cent provide a measure of the proportion of school age children who are not enrolled at the primary level. This difference does not necessarily indicate the percentage of students who are not enrolled, since some chil-

dren might be enrolled at other levels of education.

METHOD OF COMPUTATION

The indicator is calculated as the number of enrolled students within the appropriate age cohort according to school records as reported to ministries of education, divided by the number of children of primary school age.

DATA COLLECTION AND SOURCE

Data on school enrolment are usually recorded by the country ministry of education or compiled from surveys and censuses. Data on the population in the official age group for the primary level are available from national statistical offices, based on population censuses and vital statistics registration. Nationally reported values will be the same as internationally reported values only if the same methods and population estimates are used.

For international comparisons and estimates of regional and global aggregates, the UNESCO Institute for Statistics regularly produces data series on school enrolment based on data reported by education ministries or national statistical offices and United Nations population estimates.

For countries for which administrative data are not available, household survey data may be used to assess school attendance rather than enrolment. Among international surveys, the Multiple Indicator Cluster Survey and Demographic and Health Surveys (and sometimes Living Standards Measurement Surveys and the Core Welfare Indicators Questionnaires in Africa) provide school attendance data.

PERIODICITY OF MEASUREMENT

Enrolment data are recorded regularly by ministries of education and are available on a yearly basis. Data derived from surveys and censuses, when administrative records on enrolment by age and sex are not available, are less frequent. Net enrolment rates produced by UNESCO are available on an annual basis for two thirds of countries, but usually one year after the reference year. The United Nations Population Division estimates population by individual years of age biannually, although estimates may be based on population censuses conducted every 10 years in most countries. Household survey data, such as those from the Multiple Indicator Cluster Survey and Demographic and Health Surveys, are available for many developing countries at regular intervals of three to five years.

GENDER ISSUES

In situations of limited resources, families make difficult choices about sending their children to school. They may perceive the value of education differently for boys and girls. Girls are more likely than boys to suffer from limited access to education, especially in rural areas. Nevertheless, where basic education is widely accepted and overall enrolment is high, girls tend to equal or outnumber boys at primary and secondary levels.

DISAGGREGATION ISSUES

Rural and urban differences are particularly important in the analysis of enrolment data owing to significant differences in school facilities, available resources, demand on children's time for work and dropout patterns. It is also important to consider disaggregation by geographical areas and social or ethnic groups. However, showing and analysing data on specific ethnic groups may be a sensitive issue in the country. Gender differences may also be more pronounced in some social and ethnic groups.

COMMENTS AND LIMITATIONS

School enrolments may be overreported for various reasons. Survey data may not reflect actual rates of attendance or dropout during the school year. Administrators may report exaggerated enrolments, especially if there is a financial incentive to do so. Children who

repeat years may mistakenly be included in the net figures. Children's ages may be inaccurately estimated or misstated. Census data may be out of date or unreliable. There may also be insufficient data on school enrolment by sex, but existing measurement problems make it difficult to assess the situation correctly.

The indicator attempts to capture the education system's coverage and efficiency, but it does not solve the problem completely. Some children fall outside the official school age because of late or early entry rather than because of grade repetition.

Enrolment data compiled by UNESCO are adjusted to be consistent with the International Standard Classification of Education, 1997 (ICSCED) and are therefore comparable across countries. National data derived from administrative records are not necessarily based on the same classification over time and may not be comparable with data for other countries, unless exactly the same classification is used. Similarly, the concepts and terms in household surveys and censuses do not necessarily remain constant over time.

REFERENCES AND INTERNATIONAL DATA COMPARISONS

▶ **ASIAN DEVELOPMENT BANK**. Gender Issues in Basic and Primary Education. In *Gender Checklist:Education*. Manila. Available from http://www.adb.org/documents/Manuals/Gender_checklists/Education.
▶ **UNITED NATIONS** (1998). *Principles and Recommendations for Population and Housing Censuses, Revision 1*. Series M, No. 67, Rev. 1, para. 2.156 Sales No. E.98.XVII.1. Available from http://unstats.un.org/unsd/pubs (A, E, F, S).
▶ **UNITED NATIONS** (2003). *Millennium Indicators Database*. Statistics Division Internet site http://millenniumindicators.un.org.
▶ **UNITED NATIONS CHILDREN'S FUND** (2003).

Monitoring Methods. New York. Internet site http:// unicef.org/reseval/methodr. html.

▸ United Nations Children's Fund (annual). *The State of the World's Children*. New York.

▸ United Nations Development Programme (2003 and annual). *Human Development Report*. New York: Oxford University Press. Available from http://hdr.undp.org .

▸ United Nations Educational, Scientific and Cultural Organization (1978). *Revised Recommendations Concerning the International Standardization of Educational Statistics*. Paris. See also *UNESCO Statistical Yearbook, 1998*, chap.2.

▸ United Nations Educational, Scientific and Cultural Organization (1997). *International Standard Classification of Education, 1997 (ISCED)*. Montreal. Available from http://www.uis.unesco.org. Path: *Core Theme Education, Technical Guides*.

▸ World Bank (2003 and annual). *World Development Indicators*. Print and CD-ROM. Washington, D.C. Available in part from http://www.worldbank.org/data .

UNESCO data since 1998 follow the 1997 version of the International Standard Classification of Education, 1997 ISCED, which enables international comparability between countries. The time series data before 1998 are not consistent with data for 1998 and after.

AGENCIES

Ministries of education
UNESCO Institute for Statistics

7 PROPORTION OF PUPILS STARTING GRADE 1 WHO REACH GRADE 5

DEFINITION

The proportion of pupils starting grade 1 who reach grade 5, known as the survival rate to grade 5, is the percentage of a cohort of pupils enrolled in grade 1 of the primary level of education in a given school year who are expected to reach grade 5.

GOAL AND TARGET ADDRESSED

Goal 2. Achieve universal primary education
Target 3. Ensure that, by 2015, children everywhere, boys and girls alike, will be able to complete a full course of primary schooling

RATIONALE

The indicator measures an education system's success in retaining students from one grade to the next as well as its internal efficiency. Various factors account for poor performance on this indicator, including low quality of schooling, discouragement over poor performance and the direct and indirect costs of schooling. Students' progress to higher grades may also be limited by the availability of teachers, classrooms and educational materials.

METHOD OF COMPUTATION

The indicator is typically estimated from data on enrolment and repetition by grade for two consecutive years, in a procedure called the reconstructed cohort method. This method makes three assumptions: dropouts never return to school; promotion, repetition and dropout rates remain constant over the entire period in which the cohort is enrolled in school; and the same rates apply to all pupils enrolled in a given grade, regardless of whether they previously repeated a grade.

The calculation is made by dividing the total number of pupils belonging to a school cohort who reach each successive grade of the specified level of education by the number of pupils in the school cohort (in this case students originally enrolled in grade 1 of primary education) and multiplying the result by 100.

When estimated from household survey data, the proportion is estimated as the product of the proportions of transition for each grade up to grade 5. The estimation follows the method of the United Nations Educational, Scientific and Cultural Organization (UNESCO).

DATA COLLECTION AND SOURCE

The indicator proposed by the UNESCO Institute for Statistics is based on grade-specific enrolment data for two successive years for a country and on grade repeater data.

Household survey data are obtained from Multiple Indicator Cluster Surveys and Demographic and Health Surveys in a standard way and include information on current and last year school grade and level of attendance.

PERIODICITY OF MEASUREMENT

Where the data are available, they are published annually about two years after the reference year. Household surveys, such as Multiple Indicator Cluster Surveys and Demographic and Health Surveys, are generally conducted every three to five years.

GENDER ISSUES

Frequency and dropout patterns vary between girls and boys. Reasons for leaving school also differ for girls and boys and by age. Families' demand on children's time to help in household-based work is an important factor and is often greater for girls. Also important for girls are security, the proximity of school facilities and the availability of adequate sanitation and other services in schools.

DISAGGREGATION ISSUES

Rural and urban differences are particularly important in the analysis of education data, owing to significant differences in school facilities, available resources, demand on children's time for work, and dropout patterns. It is also important to consider disaggregation by geographical area and social or ethnic groups. However, showing and analysing data on specific ethnic groups may be a sensitive issue in the country. Gender differences may also be more pronounced in some social and ethnic groups.

COMMENTS AND LIMITATIONS

The method of computation has limits in measuring the degree to which school entrants survive through primary education because flows caused by new entrants, re-entrants, grade skipping, migration or transfers during the school year are not considered.

Wherever possible, the indicator should be complemented by the grade 1 intake rate, because together the indicators give a much better sense of the proportion of children in the population who complete primary education.

REFERENCES AND INTERNATIONAL DATA COMPARISONS

▸ UNITED NATIONS (1998). *Principles and Recommendations for Population and Housing Censuses, Revision 1*, Series M, No. 67, Rev. 1, para. 2.156. Sales No. E.98.XVII.1. Available from http://unstats. un.org/unsd/pubs . (A, E, F, S)

▸ UNITED NATIONS (2001). *Indicators of Sustainable Development: Guidelines and Methodologies*. Department of Economic and Social Affairs, Division for Sustainable Development. Sales No. E.01.II.A.6. Available from http://www.un.org/esa/ sustdev/natlinfo/indicators/isd.htm .

▸ UNITED NATIONS (2003). *Millennium Indicators Database*. Statistics Division Internet site http://millenniumindicators. un.org.

▸ UNITED NATIONS CHILDREN'S FUND (2000). *Monitoring Progress toward the Goals of the World Summit for Children: The End-Decade Multiple Indicator Survey Manual*. New York. Available at http://www.unicef. org/reseval/methodr.html.

▸ UNITED NATIONS CHILDREN'S FUND (annual). *The State of the World's Children*. New York.

▸ UNITED NATIONS DEVELOPMENT PROGRAMME (2003 and annual). *Human Development Report*. New York: Oxford University Press. Available at http://hdr.undp.org .

▸ UNITED NATIONS EDUCATIONAL, SCIENTIFIC AND CULTURAL ORGANIZATION (1978). *Revised Recommendations concerning the International Standardization of Educational Statistics*. Paris. Also contained in *UNESCO*

Statistical Yearbook 1998, chap.2.

▶ UNITED NATIONS EDUCATIONAL, SCIENTIFIC AND CULTURAL ORGANIZATION (1997). *International Standard Classification of Education, 1997 (ISCED)*. Montreal. Available at http://www.uis.unesco.org. Select: Core Themes/Education/Technical Guides.

▶ UNITED NATIONS EDUCATIONAL, SCIENTIFIC AND CULTURAL ORGANIZATION (2003). *Education for All: Year 2000 Assessment, Technical Guidelines*. Paris. Available at http://www.unescobkk.org/infores/efa2000/tech.htm.

▶ UNITED NATIONS EDUCATIONAL, SCIENTIFIC AND CULTURAL ORGANIZATION (2003). *World Education Indicators*. Internet site http://www.uis.unesco.org/en/stats/statistics/indicators/indic0.htm. Montreal.

▶ WORLD BANK (2003 and annual). *World Development Indicators*. Print and CD-ROM. Washington, D.C. Available in part from http://www.worldbank.org/data.

Comparable survival rates are produced by UNESCO for about 40 per cent of countries based on data from national administrative records. The number of countries reporting data for this indicator has increased over time in part because of recent inclusion of estimates obtained from household surveys such as Multiple Indicator Cluster Surveys and Demographic and Health Surveys.

AGENCIES
Ministries of education
UNESCO Institute for Statistics

7·A PRIMARY COMPLETION RATE

DEFINITION
Primary completion rate is the ratio of the total number of students successfully completing (or graduating from) the last year of primary school in a given year to the total number of children of official graduation age in the population.

GOAL AND TARGET ADDRESSED
Goal 2. Achieve universal primary education
Target 3. Ensure that, by 2015, children everywhere, boys and girls alike, will be able to complete a full course of primary schooling

RATIONALE
The indicator, which monitors education system coverage and student progression, is intended to measure human capital formation and school system quality and efficiency.

The indicator focuses on the share of children who ever complete the cycle; it is not a measure of "on-time" primary completion. Various factors may lead to poor performance on this indicator, including low quality of schooling, discouragement over poor performance and the direct and indirect costs of schooling. Students' progress to higher grades may also be limited by the availability of teachers, classrooms and educational materials.

METHOD OF COMPUTATION
The numerator may include over-age children who have repeated one or more grades of primary school but are now graduating successfully. For countries where the number of primary graduates is not reported, a proxy primary completion rate is calculated as the ratio of the total number of students in the final year of primary school, minus the number of students who repeat the grade in a typical year, to the total number of children of official graduation age in the population.

DATA COLLECTION AND SOURCE

The indicator is compiled by staff in the Education Group of the World Bank's Human Development Network based on two basic data sources used to compute gross and net enrolment ratios: enrolment data from national ministries of education and population data from the UNESCO Institute for Statistics. The World Bank and the UNESCO Institute for Statistics are committed to monitoring this indicator annually in the future.

PERIODICITY OF MEASUREMENT

Annual.

GENDER ISSUES

More understanding is needed on the patterns of completion by gender.

DISAGGREGATION ISSUES

Rural and urban differences are particularly important in the analysis of education data owing to significant differences in school facilities, available resources, demand on children's time for work and dropout patterns. It is also important to consider disaggregation by geographical area and social or ethnic groups. However, showing and analysing data on specific ethnic groups may be a sensitive issue in the country. Gender differences may also be more pronounced in some social and ethnic groups.

COMMENTS AND LIMITATIONS

The indicator reflects the primary school cycle as nationally defined according to the International Standard Classification of Education, as is the case for gross and net enrolment ratios.

While the World Bank and the UNESCO Institute for Statistics are committed to monitoring this indicator annually, systems for collecting and standardizing the data from 155 developing countries are not yet in place. As a result, the current database has many gaps, particularly for small countries, earlier years and gender breakdowns, as well as obvious anomalies and estimates that are suspect. The current database is a mixture of enrolment data and data based on different systems of graduation (examinations, diplomas, automatic promotion), limiting international comparability.

The indicator captures the final output of the primary education system, so responses to policy changes will register only with time.

The age-specific estimates are less reliable than overall population estimates. This is particularly an issue in countries with relatively rapid changes in population and its age and sex distribution resulting from such causes as internal and international migration, civil unrest and displacement. When age-specific population breakdowns are not available, the primary completion rate cannot be estimated.

Primary completion rates based on primary enrolment have an upward bias, since they do not capture those who drop out during the final grade. This implies that once the data on actual graduates become available for a country, the completion rate of the country would appear to decline.

REFERENCES AND INTERNATIONAL DATA COMPARISONS

▶ UNITED NATIONS EDUCATIONAL, SCIENTIFIC AND CULTURAL ORGANIZATION (1997). *International Standard Classification of Education, 1997 (ISCED)*. Montreal. Available at http://www.uis.unesco.org. Select: Core Themes/Education/Technical Guides.
▶ WORLD BANK (2003). *Millennium Development Goals: Achieve universal primary education*. Internet site http://www.developmentgoals.org/Education.htm. Washington, D.C.

AGENCIES

Ministries of education
UNESCO Institute for Statistics
World Bank

8 LITERACY RATE OF 15–24 YEAR-OLDS

DEFINITION

Literacy rate of 15–24 year-olds, or the youth literacy rate, is the percentage of the population 15–24 years old who can both read and write with understanding a short simple statement on everyday life. The definition of literacy sometimes extends to basic arithmetic and other life skills.

GOAL AND TARGET ADDRESSED

Goal 2. Achieve universal primary education
Target 3. Ensure that, by 2015, children everywhere, boys and girls alike, will be able to complete a full course of primary schooling

RATIONALE

The youth literacy rate reflects the outcomes of primary education over the previous 10 years or so. As a measure of the effectiveness of the primary education system, it is often seen as a proxy measure of social progress and economic achievement. The literacy rate for this analysis is simply the complement of the illiteracy rate. It is not a measure of the quality and adequacy of the literacy level needed for individuals to function in a society. Reasons for failing to achieve the literacy standard may include low quality of schooling, difficulties in attending school or dropping out before reaching grade 5.

METHOD OF COMPUTATION

The usual method of computation is to divide the number of people ages 15–24 who are literate by the total population in the same age group and to multiply the total by 100. Since literacy data are not always available for all countries and all censuses, the UNESCO Institute for Statistics uses modeling techniques to produce annual estimates based on literacy information obtained from national censuses and surveys.

DATA COLLECTION AND SOURCE

Literacy data may be derived from population censuses, household surveys and literacy surveys, and total population is derived from national censuses or sample surveys. However, not all censuses or surveys include specific questions for assessing literacy. In some countries where literacy questions are not included, a person's educational attainment (years of schooling completed) is used to assess literacy status. A common practice is to consider those with no schooling as illiterate and those who have attended grade 5 of primary school as literate.

Many household surveys, including the Multiple Indicator Cluster Surveys, Demographic and Health Surveys, Core Welfare Indicators Questionnaires in Africa and Living Standards Measurement Studies, collect literacy data, which can provide complementary data for countries without a recent census. However, definitions are not necessarily standardized (see "COMMENTS AND LIMITATIONS").

Most of the available data on literacy are based on reported literacy rather than on tested literacy and in some cases are derived from other proxy information.

PERIODICITY OF MEASUREMENT

Youth literacy rates may change more quickly than adult literacy rates and therefore need to be measured more often. Since population censuses normally occur only every 10 years, input from more frequently administered labour force and household surveys are used for annual estimates. Data are available for consecutive five-year age cohorts starting at 15–19 years old. Household surveys are generally conducted every three to five years in most developing countries.

GENDER ISSUES

Higher illiteracy rates for women are the result of lower school enrolment and early dropouts. Moreover, because women generally have less access to information and training and literacy programmes, estimates based on enrolments may overestimate literacy for girls.

DISAGGREGATION ISSUES

Rural and urban differences are particularly important in the analysis of education data because of significant differences in school facilities, available resources, demand on children's time for work and dropout patterns. It is also important to consider disaggregation by geographical area and social or ethnic groups. However, showing and analysing data on specific ethnic groups may be a sensitive issue in the country. Gender differences may also be more pronounced in some social and ethnic groups.

COMMENTS AND LIMITATIONS

Measurements of literacy can vary from simply asking "Are you literate or not?" to testing to assess literacy skills. In some cases, literacy is measured crudely in population censuses, either through self-declaration or by assuming that people with no schooling are illiterate. This causes difficulty for international comparisons. Comparability over time, even for the same survey, may also be a problem because definitions of literacy used in the surveys are not standardized. The latest revision of *Principles and Recommendations for Population and Housing Censuses* advises countries against adopting a proxy measurement based on educational attainment. It recommends that literacy questions be administered as part of national censuses and household surveys, or as part of a post-census sample enumeration.

Shortcomings in the definition of literacy, measurement problems and infrequency of censuses and literacy surveys weaken this indicator as a means of monitoring education outcomes related to the goal of achieving universal primary education.

REFERENCES AND INTERNATIONAL DATA COMPARISONS

- UNITED NATIONS (1998). *Principles and Recommendations for Population and Housing Censuses, Revision 1*, Series M, No. 67, Rev. 1. Sales No. E.98.XVII.1. Available from http://unstats. un.org/unsd/pubs (A, E, F, S).
- UNITED NATIONS (2001). *Indicators of Sustainable Development: Guidelines and Methodologies*. Sales No. E.01.II.A.6. Available from http://www.un.org/esa/ sustdev/natlinfo/indicators/isd.htm.
- UNITED NATIONS (2003). *Millennium Indicators Database*. Statistics Division Internet site http://millenniumindicators.un.org.
- UNITED NATIONS CHILDREN'S FUND (annual). *The State of the World's Children*. New York.
- UNITED NATIONS DEVELOPMENT PROGRAMME (2003 and annual). *Human Development Report*. New York: Oxford University Press. Available at http://hdr.undp.org.
- UNITED NATIONS EDUCATIONAL, SCIENTIFIC AND CULTURAL ORGANIZATION (1978). *Revised Recommendations concerning the International Standardization of Educational Statistics*. Paris. See also *UNESCO Statistical Yearbook, 1998*, chap. 2.
- UNITED NATIONS EDUCATIONAL, SCIENTIFIC AND CULTURAL ORGANIZATION (2003). *Education for All: The Year 2000 Assessment: Technical Guidelines*. Paris. Available from http://www.unescobkk.org/infores/ efa2000/tech.htm .
- UNITED NATIONS EDUCATIONAL, SCIENTIFIC AND CULTURAL ORGANIZATION (2003). *UNESCO Institute for Statistics*. Internet site http://www.uis.unesco.org. Montreal.
- WORLD BANK (2003 and annual). *World Development Indicators*. Print and CD-ROM. Washington, D.C. Available in part from http://www.worldbank.org/data.

The main international source of data is the UNESCO international data series of annual and projected estimates based on information from national population censuses and labour force, household and other surveys. The estimates are available for approximately 130 countries.

AGENCIES

Ministries of education
National statistical offices
UNESCO Institute for Statistics

9 RATIO OF GIRLS TO BOYS IN PRIMARY, SECONDARY AND TERTIARY EDUCATION

DEFINITION

Ratio of girls to boys in primary, secondary and tertiary education is the ratio of the number of female students enrolled at primary, secondary and tertiary levels in public and private schools to the number of male students.

GOAL AND TARGET ADDRESSED

Goal 3. Promote gender equality and empower women

Target 4. Eliminate gender disparity in primary and secondary education preferably by 2005, and in all levels of education no later than 2015

RATIONALE

The indicator of equality of educational opportunity, measured in terms of school enrolment, is a measure of both fairness and efficiency. Education is one of the most important aspects of human development. Eliminating gender disparity at all levels of education would help to increase the status and capabilities of women. Female education is also an important determinant of economic development.

METHOD OF COMPUTATION

The indicator is a ratio of the number of enrolled girls to enrolled boys, regardless of ages.

DATA COLLECTION AND SOURCE

Data on school enrolment are usually recorded by the ministry of education or derived from surveys and censuses. If administrative data are not available, household survey data may be used, although household surveys usually measure self-reported attendance rather than enrolment as reported by schools. Among international surveys, Multiple Indicator Cluster Surveys and Demographic and Health Surveys (and sometimes also Living Standards Measurement Studies and Core Welfare Indicators Questionnaires in Africa) provide school attendance data.

For international comparison and estimation of regional and global aggregates, the UNESCO Institute for Statistics data series on school enrolment can be used. The series is based on data reported by education ministries or national agencies for enrolment.

UNESCO produces ratios of girls to boys at country, regional and global levels for use in monitoring the Millennium Development Goals. They are available at the Millennium Indicators web site http://millenniumindicators.un.org.

PERIODICITY OF MEASUREMENT

Where official enrolment data are available, estimates from UNESCO are normally available annually about one year after the reference year. Data from household surveys may be available for selected countries at various intervals.

Official data on higher education are not as frequently reported as data on primary and secondary enrolment.

GENDER ISSUES

In situations of limited resources, families make difficult choices about sending their children to school. They may perceive the value of education differently for boys and girls. Girls are more likely than boys to suffer from limited access to education, especially in rural areas. However, where basic education is widely accepted and overall enrolment is high, girls tend to equal or outnumber boys at the primary and secondary levels. The pattern is similar in higher education, but with larger differences between the two genders.

COMMENTS AND LIMITATIONS

Some 50 countries have no system of higher education. Private education tends to be underreported, but international coverage has improved over the last four cycles of the UNESCO Institute for Statistics survey. Household survey data may include higher and private education, but may not be comparable between surveys.

The indicator is an imperfect measure of the accessibility of schooling for girls because it does not allow a determination of whether improvements in the ratio reflect increases in girls' school attendance (desirable) or decreases in boys' attendance (undesirable). It also does not show whether those enrolled in school complete the relevant education cycles.

Another limitation of the indicator is that the ratio reflects the sex structure of the school-age population. When the sex ratio in the school age population deviates significantly from 1, the indicator will not adequately reflect the actual differences between girls' and boys' enrolment. This happens in countries where boys outnumber girls at younger ages.

A ratio based on net enrolment (indicator 6) or gross enrolment is a better measure for this indicator as it takes into account the population structure of the country.

REFERENCES AND INTERNATIONAL DATA COMPARISONS

▶ **UNITED NATIONS** (2003). *Millennium Indicators Database*. Statistics Division Internet site http://millenniumindicators.un.org .
▶ **UNITED NATIONS CHILDREN'S FUND** (2000). *Monitoring Progress towards the Goals of the World Summit for Children: The End-Decade Multiple Indicator Survey Manual*. New York. Available at http://www.unicef.org/reseval/methodr.html.

▶ **UNITED NATIONS CHILDREN'S FUND** (annual). *The State of the World's Children*. New York.
▶ **UNITED NATIONS DEVELOPMENT PROGRAMME** (2003 and annual). *Human Development Report*. New York: Oxford University Press. Available at http://hdr.undp.org .
▶ **UNITED NATIONS EDUCATIONAL, SCIENTIFIC AND CULTURAL ORGANIZATION** (1978). *Revised Recommendations concerning the International Standardization of Educational Statistics*. Paris. See also *UNESCO Statistical Yearbook, 1998*, chap. 2.
▶ **UNITED NATIONS EDUCATIONAL, SCIENTIFIC AND CULTURAL ORGANIZATION** (1997). *International Standard Classification of Education, 1997 (ISCED)*. Montreal. Available at http://www.uis.unesco.org. Select: Core Themes/Education/Technical Guides.
▶ **UNITED NATIONS EDUCATIONAL, SCIENTIFIC AND CULTURAL ORGANIZATION** (2003). *Education for All: The Year 2000 Assessment, Technical Guidelines*. Paris. Available at http://www.unescobkk.org/infores/efa2000/tech.htm.
▶ **UNITED NATIONS EDUCATIONAL, SCIENTIFIC AND CULTURAL ORGANIZATION** (2003). *World Education Indicators*. Internet site http://www.uis.unesco.org/en/stats/statistics/indicators/indic0.htm. Montreal.
▶ **WORLD BANK** (2003 and annual). *World Development Indicators*. Print and CD-ROM. Washington, D.C. Available in part from http://www.worldbank.org/data.

AGENCIES
Ministries of education
UNESCO Institute for Statistics

10 RATIO OF LITERATE WOMEN TO MEN, 15–24 YEARS OLD

DEFINITION
The ratio of literate women to men, 15–24 years old (literacy gender parity index) is the ratio of the female literacy rate to the male literacy rate for the age group 15–24.

GOAL AND TARGET ADDRESSED
Goal 3. Promote gender equality and empower women

Target 4. Eliminate gender disparity in primary and secondary education preferably by 2005, and in all levels of education no later than 2015

RATIONALE
The indicator measures progress towards gender equity in literacy and learning opportunities for women in relation to those for men. It also measures a presumed outcome of attending school and a key indicator of empowerment of women in society. Literacy is a fundamental skill to empower women to take control of their lives, to engage directly with authority and to gain access to the wider world of learning.

METHOD OF COMPUTATION
The indicator is derived by dividing the literacy rate of women ages 15–24 by the literacy rate of men ages 15–24.

DATA COLLECTION AND SOURCE
Literacy data may be derived from population censuses, household surveys and literacy surveys. However, not all censuses or surveys include specific questions for assessing literacy. In some countries where literacy questions are not included, a person's educational attainment (years of schooling completed) is used to assess literacy status. A common practice is to consider those with no schooling as illiterate and defining those who have attended grade 5 of primary school as literate. Many household surveys, including the Multiple Indicator Cluster Surveys, Demographic and Health Surveys, Core Welfare Indicators Questionnaires in Africa and Living Standards Measurement Surveys, collect literacy data, which can provide complementary data for countries without a recent census. However, definitions are not necessarily standardized (see "COMMENTS AND LIMITATIONS").

PERIODICITY OF MEASUREMENT
Since population censuses normally occur every 10 years, input from more frequently administered labour force, household and other surveys are used for annual estimates. Household surveys are generally conducted every three to five years in most developing countries.

GENDER ISSUES
Higher illiteracy rates for women are the result of lower school enrolment and early dropouts. Moreover, since women generally have less access to information, training and literacy programmes, estimates based on enrolments may overestimate literacy for girls.

COMMENTS AND LIMITATIONS
Measurements of literacy can vary from simply asking "Are you literate or not?" to testing to assess literacy skills. In some cases, literacy is measured crudely in population censuses, either through self-declaration or by assuming that people with no schooling are illiterate. This causes difficulty for international comparisons. Comparability over time, even for the same survey, may also be a problem because definitions of literacy used in the surveys are not standardized. The latest revision of *Principles and Recommendations for Population and Housing Censuses* advises countries against adopting a proxy measurement based on educational attainment. It recommends that literacy questions be administered as part of national censuses and household surveys or as part of a post-census sample enumeration.

Shortcomings in the definition of literacy, measurement problems and infrequency of censuses and literacy surveys weaken this indicator as a means of monitoring education outcomes related to the goal of achieving universal primary education.

REFERENCES AND INTERNATIONAL DATA COMPARISONS

▸ UNITED NATIONS (1998). *Principles and Recommendations for Population and Housing Censuses, Revision 1*, Series M, No. 67, Rev. 1, Sales No. E.98.XVII.1. Available at http://unstats. un.org/unsd/pubs. (A, E, F, S)

▸ UNITED NATIONS (2003). *Millennium Indicators Database*. Statistics Division Internet site http://millenniumindicators.un.org.

▸ UNITED NATIONS CHILDREN'S FUND (annual). *The State of the World's Children*. New York.

▸ UNITED NATIONS DEVELOPMENT PROGRAMME (2003 and annual). *Human Development Report*. New York, Oxford University Press. Available at http://hdr.undp.org.

▸ UNITED NATIONS EDUCATIONAL, SCIENTIFIC AND CULTURAL ORGANIZATION (1978). *Revised Recommendations concerning the International Standardization of Educational Statistics*. Paris. See also *UNESCO Statistical Yearbook, 1998*, chap. 2.

▸ UNITED NATIONS EDUCATIONAL, SCIENTIFIC AND CULTURAL ORGANIZATION (2003). *Education for All: The Year 2000 Assessment: Technical Guidelines*. Paris. Available at http://www. unescobkk.org/infores/efa2000/tech.htm .

▸ UNITED NATIONS EDUCATIONAL, SCIENTIFIC AND CULTURAL ORGANIZATION (2003). UNESCO Institute for Statistics Internet site http://www.uis.unesco.org. Montreal.

▸ WORLD BANK (2003 and annual). *World Development Indicators*. Print and CD-ROM. Washington, D.C. Available in part from http://www.worldbank.org/data.

The main source of international data is the United Nations Educational, Scientific and Cultural Organization's international data series of annual and projected estimates based on information from national popula-tion censuses and labour force, household and other surveys. These estimates are available for some 130 countries.

AGENCIES
Ministries of education
National statistical offices
UNESCO Institute for Statistics

11 SHARE OF WOMEN IN WAGE EMPLOYMENT IN THE NON-AGRICULTURAL SECTOR

DEFINITION
The share of women in wage employment in the non-agricultural sector is the share of female workers in the non-agricultural sector expressed as a percentage of total employment in the sector.

The *non-agricultural sector* includes industry and services. Following the International Standard Industrial Classification (ISIC) of All Economic Activities, *industry* includes mining and quarrying (including oil production), manufacturing, construction, electricity, gas and water. *Services* includes wholesale and retail trade; restaurants and hotels; transport, storage and communications; financing, insurance, real estate and business services; and community, social and personal services.

Employment refers to people above a certain age who worked or held a job during a reference period. Employment data include both full-time and part-time workers whose remuneration is determined on the basis of hours worked or number of items produced and is independent of profits or expectation of profits.

GOAL AND TARGET ADDRESSED
Goal 3. Promote gender equality and empower women
Target 4. Eliminate gender disparity in primary and secondary education preferably by 2005, and in all levels of education no later than 2015

RATIONALE

The indicator measures the degree to which labour markets are open to women in industry and service sectors, which affects not only equal employment opportunity for women but also economic efficiency through flexibility of the labour market and, therefore, the economy's ability to adapt to change.

A significant global increase over the last decade in women's share in paid employment in the non-agricultural sector indicates that working women have become more integrated into the monetary economy through participation in the formal and informal sectors. However, labour markets remain strongly segregated. In many countries, productive work under conditions of freedom, equity and human dignity is in short supply, and this disproportionately affects women. Women are much more likely than men to work as contributing family workers, without their own pay, and in the informal sector, although there are large differentials between countries and at regional and national levels, often mirroring the relative importance of agriculture.

METHOD OF COMPUTATION

The total number of women in paid employment in the non-agricultural sector is divided by the total number of people in paid employment in that same sector.

DATA COLLECTION AND SOURCES:

Data are obtained from population censuses, labour force surveys, enterprise censuses and surveys, administrative records of social insurance schemes and official estimates based on results from several of these sources. Enterprise surveys and administrative records are likely to cover only large private and public sector employers, in particular in developing countries. The other sources may cover the whole relevant population.

PERIODICITY OF MEASUREMENT:

Results from population censuses are normally available every 10 years, while estimates based on other sources may be available annually or less frequently in some developing countries.

GENDER ISSUES

There are large differences between women and men in non-agricultural employment, in particular in developing countries. This is the result of differences between rates of participation in employment for women and men as well as the kind of employment in which they participate. In many regions, women are more likely than men to be engaged in informal sector activities and subsistence or unpaid work in the household.

Wage employment in most of Africa and much of Asia and the Pacific is a middle-class, urban phenomenon. Outside of urban areas, most employment is agricultural, often for family subsistence. However, where non-agricultural employment is available, it is more likely to go to male members of the household.

As economies develop, the share of women in non-agricultural wage employment becomes increasingly important. A higher share in paid employment could secure for them better income, economic security and well-being. However, this shift is not automatic, nor does it account for differentials in working conditions between men and women. Other variables need to be considered, such as level of education, level of remuneration and wage differentials, and the extent to which women and men benefit from labour legislation and social programmes. Men more often hold regular and better remunerated jobs, whereas women are frequently in peripheral, insecure, less valued jobs, as home workers, casual workers or part-time or temporary workers.

COMMENTS AND LIMITATIONS

Although there are clear international standards for the relevant concepts, countries may use different defini tions for employment status, especially for part-time workers, students, members of the armed forces and household or contributing family workers. Also, different sources of data may use different definitions and have different coverage, with limited comparability across countries and over time within the same country. The employment share of the agricultural sector is severely underreported. In addition, studies have shown that employment activity questions on standard censuses tend to grossly underestimate the extent of female employment of any kind.

REFERENCES AND INTERNATIONAL DATA COMPARISONS

▸ **ANKER, R., M.E. KHAN** and **R.B. GUPTA** (1988). *Women's Participation in the Labour Force: A Methods Test in India for Improving Its Measurement*. Women, Work and Development 16. Geneva: International Labour Office.

▸ **INTERNATIONAL LABOUR OFFICE** (1988). *Assessing Women's Economic Contribution to Development*. Geneva.

▸ **INTERNATIONAL LABOUR OFFICE** (2002). *Women and Men in the Informal Economy: A statistical picture*. Geneva. available from http:// www.ilo.org/public/english/employment/g ems/download/women.pdf.

▸ **INTERNATIONAL LABOUR ORGANIZATION** (2000). *Current International Recommendations on Labour Statistics, 2000 Edition*. Geneva.

▸ **INTERNATIONAL LABOUR ORGANIZATION** (2003). *Laborsta—an International Labour Office database on labour statistics operated by the ILO Bureau of Statistics*. Internet site http://laborsta.ilo.org. Geneva.

▸ **INTERNATIONAL LABOUR ORGANIZATION** (annual). *Key Indicators of the Labour Market*. Geneva. Available in part from http://www.ilo. org/kilm.

▸ **INTERNATIONAL LABOUR ORGANIZATION** (annual). *Yearbook of Labour Statistics*. Geneva. Available at http://laborsta.ilo.org .

▸ **SWEDEN, STATISTICS SWEDEN** (1996). *Engendering Statistics: A Tool for Change*. Stockholm.

▸ **UNITED NATIONS** (1990). *International Standard Industrial Classification of All Economic Activities (ISIC)*. Series M, No. 4, Rev. 3.1. available from http://unstats.un. org/unsd/cr/registry.

▸ **UNITED NATIONS** (1998). *Principles and Recommendations for Population and Housing Censuses, Revision 1*, Series M, No. 67, Rev. 1. Sales No. E.98.XVII.1. Available from http://unstats. un.org/unsd/pubs. (A, E, F, S)

▸ **UNITED NATIONS** (2003). *Millennium Indicators Database*. Statistics Division Internet site http://millenniumindicators.un.org.

▸ **WORLD BANK** (2003 and annual). *World Development Indicators*. Print and CD-ROM. Washington, D.C. Available in part from http://www.worldbank.org/data .

International data are compiled by the International Labour Organization based on data reported by countries. An increasing number of countries report economic activity according to the ISIC.

AGENCIES
Ministries of labour
National statistical offices
International Labour Organization

12 PROPORTION OF SEATS HELD BY WOMEN IN NATIONAL PARLIAMENTS

DEFINITION
The *proportion of seats held by women in national parliaments* is the number of seats held by women expressed as a percentage of all occupied seats.

GOAL AND TARGET ADDRESSED
Goal 3. Promote gender equality and empower women
Target 4. Eliminate gender disparity in primary and secondary education preferably by 2005, and in all levels of education no later than 2015

RATIONALE
Women's representation in parliaments is one aspect of women's opportunities in political and public life, and it is therefore linked to women's empowerment.

METHOD OF COMPUTATION

The indicator is obtained by dividing the number of parliamentary seats occupied by women by the total number of seats occupied. National parliaments consist of one or two chambers. For international comparisons, generally only the single or lower house is considered in calculating the indicator.

DATA COLLECTION AND SOURCE

At the national level, the data come from the records of national parliaments. National parliaments also report the total number of parliamentary seats and the number occupied by women and men to the Inter-Parliamentary Union (IPU), which regularly compiles international data series and global and regional aggregates.

PERIODICITY OF MEASUREMENT

The data are commonly available from national parliaments and updated after an election. National parliaments also transmit their data to the IPU at least once a year and when the numbers change significantly, such as after an election.

GENDER ISSUES

Women are underrepresented in all decision-making bodies and within political parties, particularly at the higher echelons. Women still face many practical obstacles to the full exercise of their role in political life.

COMMENTS AND LIMITATIONS

Parliaments vary considerably in their independence and authority, though they generally engage in law-making, oversight of Government and representation of the electorate. In terms of measuring women's real political decision-making, this indicator may not be sufficient, because women still face many obstacles in fully and efficiently carrying out their parliamentary mandate. Thus, being a member of parliament, especially in developing countries and emerging democracies, does not guarantee that a woman has the resources, respect or constituency to exercise significant influence.

REFERENCES AND INTERNATIONAL DATA COMPARISONS

▶ INTER-PARLIAMENTARY UNION (2003). *Women in National Parliaments*. Internet site http://www.ipu.org/wmn-e/world.htm. Geneva.
▶ UNITED NATIONS (2003). *Millennium Indicators Database*. Statistics Division Internet site http://millenniumindicators.un.org.
▶ UNITED NATIONS DEVELOPMENT FUND FOR WOMEN (2000). *Progress of the World's Women*. New York. available from http://www.unifem.undp.org/progressww/2000.
▶ UNITED NATIONS DEVELOPMENT PROGRAMME (2003 and annual). *Human Development Report*. New York: Oxford University Press. Available at http://hdr.undp.org.

The IPU regularly compiles international data series and global and regional aggregates.

AGENCIES

National parliaments
Inter-Parliamentary Union

13 UNDER-FIVE MORTALITY RATE

DEFINITION

The *under-five mortality rate* is the probability (expressed as a rate per 1,000 live births) of a child born in a specified year dying before reaching the age of five if subject to current age-specific mortality rates.

GOAL AND TARGET ADDRESSED

Goal 4. Reduce child mortality
Target 5. Reduce by two thirds, between 1990 and 2015, the under-five mortality rate

RATIONALE

The indicator, which relates directly to the target, measures child survival. It also reflects the social, economic and environmental conditions in which children (and others in society) live, including their health care. Because data on the incidences and prevalence of diseases (morbidity data) frequently are unavailable, mortality rates are often used to identify vulnerable populations. The under-five mortality rate captures more than 90 per cent of global mortality among children under the age of 18.

METHOD OF COMPUTATION

Age-specific mortality rates are calculated from data on births and deaths in vital statistics registries, censuses and household surveys in developing countries. Estimates based on household survey data are obtained directly (using birth history, as in Demographic and Health Surveys) or indirectly (Brass method, as in Multiple Indicator Cluster Surveys). The data are then summed for children under five, and the results are expressed as a rate per 1,000 live births.

DATA COLLECTION AND SOURCE

At the national level, the best source of data is a complete vital statistics registration system—one covering at least 90 per cent of vital events in the population. Such systems are uncommon in developing countries, so estimates are also obtained from sample surveys or derived by applying direct and indirect estimation techniques to registration, census or survey data. A wide variety of household surveys, including Multiple Indicator Cluster Surveys and Demographic and Health Surveys, are used in developing countries.

Several international agencies produce country estimates based on available national data for purposes of international comparisons and assessment of global and regional trends (see below, "International data comparisons").

PERIODICITY OF MEASUREMENT

Vital statistics are typically available once a year, but they are unreliable in most develop-

ing countries. Household surveys that include questions on births and deaths are generally conducted every three to five years.

GENDER ISSUES

Under-five mortality rates are higher for boys than for girls in countries without significant parental gender preferences. Under-five mortality better captures the effect of gender discrimination than infant mortality, as nutrition and medical interventions are more important in this age group, while biological differences have a higher impact during the first year of life (see also indicator 14, infant mortality rate). There may be gender-based biases in the reporting of child deaths.

DISAGGREGATION ISSUES

Under-five mortality generally shows large disparities across geographical areas and between rural and urban areas. Under-five mortality may also vary across socio-economic groups. Children in some ethnic groups might also be at higher risk of malnutrition, poorer health and higher mortality. However, showing and analysing data on specific ethnic groups may be a sensitive issue in the country. Gender differences may also be more pronounced in some social and ethnic groups.

COMMENTS AND LIMITATIONS

Data on under-five mortality is more complete and more timely than data on adult mortality. The under-five mortality rate is considered to be a more robust estimate than the infant mortality rate if the information is drawn from household surveys.

In developing countries, household surveys are essential to the calculation of the indicator, but there are some limits to their quality. Survey data are subject to recall error; in addition, surveys estimating under-five deaths require large samples because such incidences are uncommon and representative households cannot ordinarily be identified for sampling. Moreover, the frequency of the survey is generally only every three to five years. Therefore, when using household surveys it is important to take sampling errors into account. In addition, indirect estimates rely on estimated actuarial ("life") tables that may be inappropriate for the population concerned.

There are also gender-based biases in the reporting of child deaths.

REFERENCES AND INTERNATIONAL DATA COMPARISONS

▸ UNITED NATIONS (2001). *Indicators of Sustainable Development: Guidelines and Methodologies*. Sales No. E.01.II.A.6. Available from http://www.un.org/esa/sustdev/natlinfo/indicators/isd.htm .

▸ UNITED NATIONS (2001). *Principles and Recommendations for a Vital Statistics System, Revision 2*. Series M, No. 19, Rev. 2. Sales No. 01.XVII.10. Available from http://unstats.un.org/unsd/pubs.

▸ UNITED NATIONS (2003 and biennial). *World Population Prospects: The 2002 Revision*, vol. 1. *Comprehensive Tables* (Sales No. E.03.XIII.6) and vol. 2, *Sex and Age distribution of the World Population* (Sales No. E.03.XIII.7). Available from http://esa.un.org/unpp.

▸ UNITED NATIONS CHILDREN'S FUND (2000). *Monitoring Progress towards the Goals of the World Summit for Children: The End-Decade Multiple Indicator Survey Manual*. New York. Available from http://www.unicef. org/reseval/methodr.html .

▸ UNITED NATIONS CHILDREN'S FUND (annual). *The State of the World's Children*. New York.

▸ UNITED NATIONS DEVELOPMENT PROGRAMME (2003 and annual). *Human Development Report*. New York: Oxford University Press. available from http://hdr.undp.org .

▸ WORLD BANK (2003 and annual). *World Development Indicators*. Print and CD-ROM. Washington, D.C. Available in part from http://www.worldbank.org/data .

▸ WORLD HEALTH ORGANIZATION (1992). *International Statistical Classification of Diseases and Related Health Problems,* *Tenth Revision (ICD-10)*, vol. 1. Geneva.

▸ WORLD HEALTH ORGANIZATION (2003). *WHO Statistical Information System (WHOSIS)— Evidence and Information for Health Policy*. Internet site http://www3.who.int/whosis/menu.cfm. Geneva.

Mortality rates are among the most frequently used indicators to compare levels of socio-economic development across countries. The United Nations Population Division, the United Nations Children's Fund and the World Health Organization regularly produce estimates of under-five mortality based on available national data. The data series may differ, however, owing to differences in methodologies used to estimate data and differences in reporting periods.

AGENCIES
Ministries of health
National statistical offices
United Nations Children's Fund
World Health Organization

 ## 14 INFANT MORTALITY RATE

DEFINITION
The *infant mortality rate* is typically defined as the number of infants dying before reaching the age of one year per 1,000 live births in a given year.

GOAL AND TARGET ADDRESSED
Goal 4. Reduce child mortality
Target 5. Reduce by two-thirds, between 1990 and 2015, the under-five mortality rate

RATIONALE
Although the target relates specifically to under-five mortality, infant mortality is relevant to the monitoring of the target since it represents an important component of under-five mortality.

Infant mortality rates measure child survival. They also reflect the social, economic and environmental conditions in which children (and others in society) live, including their health care. Since data on the incidence and prevalence of diseases (morbidity data) frequently are unavailable, mortality rates are often used to identify vulnerable populations.

METHOD OF COMPUTATION

The indicator is the number of deaths of infants under one year of age in the indicated year per 1,000 live births in the same year.

For data from vital statistics registrations (when reliable), the number of live births and deaths in the same year of children under one year old are estimated. The number of deaths is divided by the number of births and the result is multiplied by 1,000.

For data from household surveys, infant mortality estimates are obtained directly (using birth history, as in Demographic and Health Surveys) or indirectly (Brass method, as in Multiple Indicator Cluster Surveys). When estimated indirectly, the under-one mortality estimates must be consistent with the under-five mortality estimates.

DATA COLLECTION AND SOURCE

The best source of data is a complete vital statistics registration system—one covering at least 90 per cent of vital events in the population. Such systems are uncommon in developing countries, so estimates are also obtained from sample surveys or derived by applying direct and indirect estimation techniques to registration, census or survey data. A wide variety of household surveys, including Multiple Indicator Cluster Surveys and Demographic and Health Surveys, are used in developing countries.

PERIODICITY OF MEASUREMENT

Vital statistics are typically available once a year, but they are unreliable in most developing countries. Household surveys that include questions on births and deaths are usually conducted every three to five years.

GENDER ISSUES

Girls have a survival advantage over boys during the first year of life, largely based on biological differences. This is especially so during the first month of life when perinatal conditions are most likely to be the cause or a contributing cause of death. While infant mortality is generally higher for boys than for girls, in some countries girls' biological advantage is outweighed by gender-based discrimination (see also INDICATOR 13, "Under-five mortality rate"). However, under-five mortality better captures the effect of gender discrimination than infant mortality, as nutrition and medical interventions are more important after age one.

DISAGGREGATION ISSUES

Infant mortality generally shows large disparities across geographical areas and between urban and rural areas. Infant mortality may also vary across socioeconomic groups, and the indicator is often used as a general indicator of social distress in populations. Infants in some ethnic groups might also be at higher risk of malnutrition, poorer health and higher mortality. However, showing and analysing data on specific ethnic groups may be a sensitive issue in the country. Gender differences may also be more pronounced in some social and ethnic groups.

COMMENTS AND LIMITATIONS

The infant mortality rate is considered to be a more robust estimate than the under-five mortality rate if the information is drawn from vital statistics registration.

In developing countries, household surveys are essential to the calculation of the indicator, but there are some limits to their quality. Survey data are subject to recall error, and surveys estimating infant deaths require large samples because such incidences are uncommon and representative households cannot ordinarily be identified for sampling. Moreover, the frequency of the surveys is generally only every three to five years. Therefore, when using household survey estimates, it is important to take sampling errors into account.

REFERENCES AND INTERNATIONAL DATA COMPARISONS

▸ UNITED NATIONS (1958). *Multilingual Demographic Dictionary.* Population Studies, No. 29. Sales No. E.58.XIII.4.

▸ UNITED NATIONS (1999). *World Population Prospects: The 1998 Revision*, vol. III, *Analytical Report.* Sales No. E.99.XIII.10.

▸ UNITED NATIONS (2001). *Principles and Recommendations for a Vital Statistics System, Revision 2.* Series M, No. 19, Rev. 2. Sales No. 01.XVII.10. Available from http:// unstats.un. org/unsd/pubs.

▸ UNITED NATIONS (2003 and biennial). *World Population Prospects: The 2002 Revision*, vol. 1. *Comprehensive Tables* (Sales No. E.03.XIII.6) and vol. 2, *Sex and Age distribution of the World Population.* (Sales No. E.03.XIII.7). Available from http://esa. un.org/unpp.

▸ UNITED NATIONS CHILDREN'S FUND (annual). *The State of the World's Children.* New York.

▸ UNITED NATIONS DEVELOPMENT PROGRAMME (2003 and annual). *Human Development Report.* New York: Oxford University Press. available from http://hdr.undp.org .

▸ WORLD BANK (2003 and annual). *World Development Indicators.* Print and CD-ROM. Washington, D.C. Available in part from http://www.worldbank.org/data .

▸ WORLD HEALTH ORGANIZATION (1992). *International Statistical Classification of Diseases and Related Health Problems, Tenth Revision (ICD-10)*, vol.1. Geneva.

▸ WORLD HEALTH ORGANIZATION (2003). *WHO Statistical Information System (WHOSIS)— Evidence and Information for Health Policy.* Internet site http://www3.who.int/whosis/ menu.cfm . Geneva.

Mortality rates are among the most frequently used indicators to compare levels of socio-economic development across countries. The United Nations Population Division, the United Nations Children's Fund and the World Health Organization regularly produce estimates of infant and under-five mortality based on available national data. The data series may differ, however, owing to differences in methodologies used to estimate data and differences in reporting periods.

AGENCIES
Ministries of health
National statistical offices
United Nations Children's Fund
World Health Organization

15 PROPORTION OF 1-YEAR-OLD CHILDREN IMMUNIZED AGAINST MEASLES

DEFINITION
The *proportion of 1-year-old children immunized against measles* is the percentage of children under one year of age who have received at least one dose of measles vaccine.

GOAL AND TARGET ADDRESSED
Goal 4. Reduce child mortality
Target 5. Reduce by two thirds, between 1990 and 2015, the under-five mortality rate

RATIONALE
The indicator provides a measure of the coverage and the quality of the child health-care system in the country. Immunization is an essential component for reducing under-five mortality. Governments in developing countries usually finance immunization against measles and diphtheria, pertussis (whooping cough) and tetanus (DPT) as part of the basic health package. Among these vaccine-preventable diseases of childhood, measles is the leading cause of child mortality. Health and other programmes targeted at those specific causes are one practical means of reducing child mortality.

METHOD OF COMPUTATION

The indicator is estimated as the percentage of children ages 12–23 months who received at least one dose of measles vaccine either any time before the survey or before the age of 12 months. Estimates of immunization coverage are generally based on two sources of empirical data: administrative data and coverage surveys (see "Data collection and sources"). For estimates based on administrative data, immunization coverage is derived by dividing the total number of vaccinations by the number of children in the target population. For most vaccines, the target population is the national annual number of births or number of surviving infants (this may vary depending on a country's policies and the specific vaccine). Immunization coverage surveys are frequently used in connection with administrative data.

DATA COLLECTION AND SOURCE

The two sources available at the national level are reports of vaccinations performed by service providers (administrative data) and household surveys containing information on children's vaccination history (coverage surveys). The principle types of surveys used as sources of information on immunization coverage are Expanded Programme on Immunization (EPI) 30 cluster surveys, Multiple Indicator Cluster Surveys and Demographic and Health Surveys. Routine data are compiled by national EPI programme managers.

The World Health Organization and the United Nations Children's Fund compile country data series based on both types of data, gathered through the WHO/UNICEF Joint Reporting Form on Vaccine-Preventable Diseases.

PERIODICITY OF MEASUREMENT

Administrative data are collected annually. Surveys are generally conducted every three to five years.

GENDER ISSUES

Immunization programmes are generally free of charge and should not discriminate between boys and girls. However, in some countries of south-central Asia and northern Africa, girls' immunization rates are lower than boys', probably due to cultural rather than economic reasons.

COMMENTS AND LIMITATIONS

The first dose of measles vaccine is supposed to be administered to all children at the age of nine months or shortly after. By 2000, most countries were providing a "second opportunity" for measles vaccination, either through a two-dose routine schedule or through a combined routine schedule and supplementary campaigns. Measles immunization coverage is expressed as the percentage of children who have received at least one dose.

Vaccination coverage for measles needs to be above 90 per cent to stop transmission of the virus—not only because measles is so contagious, but also because up to 15 per cent of children vaccinated at nine months fail to develop immunity. Some countries in the Latin America and Caribbean region, for example, administer the measles vaccine at 12–15 months of age. This has to be taken into account in calculations of coverage based on household surveys.

In many developing countries, lack of precise information on the size of the cohort of children under one year of age makes immunization coverage difficult to estimate.

REFERENCES AND INTERNATIONAL DATA COMPARISONS

▸ GUNN, S.W.A., KLUWER ACADEMIC PUBLISHERS (1990). *Multilingual Dictionary of Disaster Medicine and International Relief*. Dordrecht, The Netherlands. English/Français/Español/Arabic.
▸ UNITED NATIONS CHILDREN'S FUND (2003). *Health*. Internet site http://www.unicef.

org/health/index.html. New York.

▶ **UNITED NATIONS CHILDREN'S FUND** (2003). *Routine Immunization*. Internet site http://www.childinfo.org/eddb/immuni/index.htm. New York.

▶ **UNITED NATIONS CHILDREN'S FUND** (annual). *The State of the World's Children*. New York.

▶ **WORLD HEALTH ORGANIZATION** (1992). *International Statistical Classification of Diseases and Related Health Problems, Tenth Revision (ICD-10)*, vol. 1. Geneva.

▶ **WORLD HEALTH ORGANIZATION** (1999). *Recommended Standards for Surveillance of Selected Vaccine-Preventable Diseases.* WHO/EPI/GEN/99012. Geneva.

▶ **WORLD HEALTH ORGANIZATION** (2003). *Measles.* Internet site http://www.who.int/health_topics/measles/en. Geneva.

▶ **WORLD HEALTH ORGANIZATION** (2003). *Surveillance.* Internet site http://www.who.int/vaccines-surveillance. Geneva.

WHO and UNICEF compile country data series based on administrative data and household surveys, gathered through the WHO/UNICEF Joint Reporting Form on Vaccine-Preventable Diseases.

AGENCIES
Ministries of health
United Nations Children's Fund
World Health Organization

 ## 16 MATERNAL MORTALITY RATIO

DEFINITION
The *maternal mortality ratio* is the number of women who die from any cause related to or aggravated by pregnancy or its management (excluding accidental or incidental causes) during pregnancy and childbirth or within 42 days of termination of pregnancy, irrespective of the duration and site of the pregnancy, per 100,000 live births. The 10th revision of the International Classification of Diseases makes

provision for including late maternal deaths occurring between six weeks and one year after childbirth.

GOAL AND TARGET ADDRESSED
Goal 5. Improve maternal health
Target 6. Reduce by three quarters, between 1990 and 2015, the maternal mortality ratio

RATIONALE
The indicator, which is directly related to the target, monitors deaths related to pregnancy. Such deaths are affected by various factors, including general health status, education and services during pregnancy and childbirth. It is important to monitor changes in health conditions related to sex and reproduction.

METHOD OF COMPUTATION
The maternal mortality ratio can be calculated by dividing recorded (or estimated) maternal deaths by total recorded (or estimated) live births in the same period and multiplying by 100,000. The indicator can be calculated directly from data collected through vital statistics registrations, household surveys or hospital studies. However, those sources all have data quality problems (see "Data collection and sources"). Alternative methods include a review of all deaths of women of reproductive age (so-called Reproductive Age Mortality Surveys, or RAMOS), longitudinal studies of pregnant women and repeated household studies. All these methods, however, still rely on accurate reporting of deaths of pregnant women and of the cause of death, something that is difficult to obtain.

Another problem is the need for large sample sizes, which raises costs. This can be overcome by using sisterhood methods. The indirect sisterhood method asks respondents four simple questions about how many of their sisters reached adulthood, how many have died and whether those who died were pregnant around the time of death. However, the reference period of the estimate is at least

10–12 years before the survey. The direct sisterhood method used in Demographic and Health Surveys also asks respondents to provide the date of death, which permits the calculation of more recent estimates, but even then the reference period tends to center on 0–6 years before the survey.

Maternal deaths should be divided into two groups. Direct obstetric deaths result from obstetric complications of the pregnant state (pregnancy, labour and puerperium); from interventions, omissions or incorrect treatment; or from a chain of events resulting from any of these. Indirect obstetric deaths result from previously existing disease or disease that developed during pregnancy and that was not directly due to obstetric causes but was aggravated by the physiologic effects of pregnancy. Published maternal mortality ratios should always specify whether the numerator (number of recorded maternal deaths) is the number of recorded direct obstetric deaths or the number of recorded obstetric deaths (direct plus indirect). Maternal deaths from HIV/AIDS and obstetrical tetanus are included in the maternal mortality ratio.

DATA COLLECTION AND SOURCE
Good vital statistics registration systems are rare in developing countries. Official data are usually obtained from health service records, but few women in rural areas have access to health services. So in developing countries, it is more usual to use survey data. The most common sources of data are the Demographic and Health Surveys and similar household surveys. Available data on levels of maternal mortality are generally significantly underestimated because of problems of misclassification and underreporting of maternal deaths. The World Health Organization, the United Nation's Children's Fund and the United Nations Population Fund have adjusted existing data to take account of these problems and have developed model-based estimates for countries with no reliable national data on maternal mortality. It is those estimates that are usually published in international tables.

PERIODICITY OF MEASUREMENT
Every 7–10 years.

GENDER ISSUES
The low social and economic status of girls and women is a fundamental determinant of maternal mortality in many countries. Low status limits the access of girls and women to education and good nutrition as well as to the economic resources needed to pay for health care or family planning services.

COMMENTS AND LIMITATIONS
The indicator is generally of unknown reliability, as are many other cause-specific mortality indicators, owing to the difficulty in distinguishing deaths that are genuinely related to pregnancy from deaths that are not. Even in industrialized countries with comprehensive vital statistics registration systems, misclassification and underreporting of maternal deaths can lead to serious underestimation. Because it is a relatively rare event, large sample sizes are needed if household surveys are used. Household surveys such as the Demographic and Health Survey attempt to measure maternal mortality by asking respondents about survivorship of sisters. While the sisterhood method reduces sample size requirements, it produces estimates covering some 6–12 years before the survey, which renders the data problematic for monitoring progress or observing the impact of interventions. In addition, owing to the very large confidence limits around the estimates, they are not suitable for assessing trends over time or for making comparisons between countries. As a result, it is recommended that process indicators, such as attendance by skilled health personnel at delivery and use of emergency obstetric care facilities, be used to assess progress towards the reduction in maternal mortality.

The maternal mortality ratio should not be confused with the maternal mortality rate (whose denominator is the number of women of reproductive age), which measures the likelihood of both becoming pregnant and dying during pregnancy or the puerperium (six weeks after delivery). The maternal mortality ratio (whose denominator is the number of live birth), takes fertility levels (likelihood of becoming pregnant) into consideration.

REFERENCES AND INTERNATIONAL DATA COMPARISONS

▶ UNITED NATIONS (2003 and biennial). *World Population Prospects: The 2002 Revision*, vol. 1. *Comprehensive Tables* (Sales No. E.03.XIII.6) and vol. 2, *Sex and Age distribution of the World Population* (Sales No. E.03.XIII.7). Available from http://esa.un.org/unpp.

▶ UNITED NATIONS (2003). *Millennium Indicators Database*. Statistics Division Internet site http://millenniumindicators.un.org.

▶ UNITED NATIONS CHILDREN'S FUND (annual). *The State of the World's Children*. New York.

▶ UNITED NATIONS DEVELOPMENT PROGRAMME (2003 and annual). *Human Development Report*. New York: Oxford University Press. Available from http://hdr.undp.org .

▶ UNITED NATIONS POPULATION FUND (1998). Issues in measuring and monitoring maternal mortality: implications for programmes. Technical and Policy Paper No.1. New York.

▶ UNITED NATIONS POPULATION FUND (annual). *State of World Population*. Available from http://www.unfpa.org/swp/swpmain.htm .

▶ WORLD BANK (2003 and annual). *World Development Indicators*. Print and CD-ROM. Washington, D.C. Available in part from http://www.worldbank.org/data .

▶ WORLD HEALTH ORGANIZATION (1991). *Maternal Mortality: A Global Factbook*. Geneva.

▶ WORLD HEALTH ORGANIZATION (1992). *International Statistical Classification of Diseases and Related Health Problems, Tenth Revision (ICD-10)*, vol. 1. Geneva.

▶ WORLD HEALTH ORGANIZATION (1999). *Reduction of Maternal Mortality: A Joint WHO/UNFPA/UNICEF/World Bank Statement*. Geneva. Available from www.who.int/reproductive-health.

▶ WORLD HEALTH ORGANIZATION, and UNITED NATIONS CHILDREN'S FUND (1997). *The Sisterhood Method for Estimating Maternal Mortality: Guidance Notes for Potential Users*. Geneva.

▶ WORLD HEALTH ORGANIZATION, UNITED NATIONS CHILDREN'S FUND and UNITED NATIONS POPULATION FUND (2001). *Maternal Mortality in 1995*. Geneva.

The World Health Organization, the United Nation's Children's Fund and the United Nations Population Fund have adjusted existing data to account for the problems and have developed model-based estimates for countries with no reliable national data on maternal mortality. It is those estimates that are usually published in international tables.

AGENCIES
Ministries of health
United Nations Children's Fund
World Health Organization
United Nations Population Fund

17 PROPORTION OF BIRTHS ATTENDED BY SKILLED HEALTH PERSONNEL

DEFINITION
The *proportion of births attended by skilled health personnel* is the percentage of deliveries attended by personnel trained to give the necessary supervision, care and advice to women during pregnancy, labour and the post-partum period; to conduct deliveries on their own; and to care for newborns.

Skilled health personnel include only those who are properly trained and who have appropriate equipment and drugs. Traditional birth attendants, even if they have received a short training course, are not to be included.

GOAL AND TARGET ADDRESSED

Goal 5. Improve maternal health

Target 6. Reduce by three quarters, between 1990 and 2015, the maternal mortality ratio

RATIONALE

Measuring maternal mortality accurately is unusually difficult, except where there is comprehensive registration of deaths and causes of death. Several process indicators have been proposed for tracking progress by focusing on professional care during pregnancy and childbirth, particularly for the management of complications. The most widely available indicator is the proportion of women who deliver with the assistance of a medically trained health-care provider.

METHOD OF COMPUTATION

The number of births attended by skilled health personnel (doctors, nurses or midwives) is expressed as a percentage of deliveries (or births if those are the only data available) in the same period.

GENDER ISSUES

The low social status of women in developing countries limits their access to economic resources and basic education and thus their ability to make decisions related to health and nutrition. Some women are denied access to care when it is needed either because of cultural practices of seclusion or because decision-making is the responsibility of other family members. Lack of access to or use of essential obstetric services is a crucial factor contributing to high maternal mortality.

PERIODICITY OF MEASUREMENT

Household survey data on this indicator is generally available every three to five years.

COMMENTS AND LIMITATIONS

The indicator is a measure of a health system's ability to provide adequate care for pregnant women. Concerns have been expressed that the term *skilled attendant* may not adequately capture women's access to good quality care, particularly when complications arise. Standardization of the definition of *skilled* health personnel is sometimes difficult because of differences in training of health personnel in different countries. Although efforts have been made to standardize the definitions of doctors, nurses and midwives and auxiliary midwives used in most household surveys, it is probable that many "skilled attendants" would not meet the criteria for a "skilled attendant" as defined by the World Health Organization. Moreover, it is clear that skilled attendants' ability to provide appropriate care in an emergency depends on the environment in which they work.

DATA COLLECTION AND SOURCE

Data are collected through household surveys, in particular Demographic and Health Surveys and Multiple Indicator Cluster Surveys, as well as other national household surveys.

REFERENCES AND INTERNATIONAL DATA COMPARISONS

▸ UNITED NATIONS (2003). *Millennium Indicators Database*. Statistics Division Internet site http://millenniumindicators. un.org.

▸ UNITED NATIONS CHILDREN'S FUND (annual). *The State of the World's Children*. New York.

▸ UNITED NATIONS DEVELOPMENT PROGRAMME (2003 and annual). *Human Development Report*. New York: Oxford University Press. Available from http://hdr.undp.org.

▸ UNITED NATIONS POPULATION FUND (annual). *State of World Population*. Available from http://www.unfpa.org/swp/swpmain.htm.

▸ WORLD BANK (2003 and annual). *World Development Indicators*. Print and CD-ROM. Washington, D.C. Available in part from http://www.worldbank.org/data.

▸ WORLD HEALTH ORGANIZATION (2001). *Reproductive Health Indicators for Global Monitoring: Report of the Second Interagency Meeting, 2001*. WHO/RHR/ 01.19. Geneva.

▶ **WORLD HEALTH ORGANIZATION** (2003). *WHO Statistical Information System (WHOSIS)— Evidence and Information for Health Policy.* Internet site http://www3.who.int/whosis/menu.cfm. Geneva.

AGENCIES
Ministries of health
United Nations Children's Fund
World Health Organization
United Nations Population Fund

18 HIV PREVALENCE AMONG PREGNANT WOMEN AGED 15–24 YEARS

DEFINITION
HIV prevalence among 15–24 year-old pregnant women is the percentage of pregnant women ages 15–24 whose blood samples test positive for HIV.

GOAL AND TARGET ADDRESSED
Goal 6. Combat HIV/AIDS, malaria and other diseases
Target 7. Have halted by 2015 and begun to reverse the spread of HIV/AIDS

RATIONALE
HIV infection leads to AIDS. Without treatment, average survival from the time of infection is about nine years. Access to treatment is uneven, and no vaccine is currently available.

About half of all new HIV cases are among people 24 years of age or younger. In generalized epidemics (with prevalence consistently at more than 1 per cent among pregnant women), the infection rate for pregnant women is similar to the overall rate for the adult population. Therefore, the indicator is a measure of the spread of the epidemic. In low-level and concentrated epidemics, HIV prevalence is monitored in groups with high-risk behaviour because prevalence among pregnant women is low.

METHOD OF COMPUTATION
The number of pregnant women whose blood samples test positive for HIV expressed as a percentage of all pregnant women in that age group whose blood is tested.

DATA COLLECTION AND SOURCE
Data on HIV in pregnant women come from tests on leftover blood samples taken for other reasons during pregnancy. The samples come from selected antenatal clinics during routine sentinel surveillance, chosen to reflect urban, rural and other socio-geographic divisions in a country. HIV prevalence data in groups with high-risk behaviour are collected in serosurveys that are part of the surveillance system or in ad hoc prevalence surveys.

Only the results of unlinked, anonymous screening of blood taken for other purposes should be used in calculating this indicator of HIV prevalence. Refusal and other forms of participation bias are considerably reduced in unlinked, anonymous HIV testing compared with other forms of testing, such as in programmes that offer counselling and voluntary HIV testing for pregnant women to reduce mother-to-child transmission.

The data are gathered by the World Health Organization and the Joint United Nations Programme on HIV/AIDS.

PERIODICITY OF MEASUREMENT
The data are collated annually in many developing countries.

GENDER ISSUES
Pregnant women are chosen for clinical surveillance, not because of gender issues, but because they offer a unique opportunity to monitor HIV/AIDS.

Throughout the world, the unequal social status of women places them at higher risk for contracting HIV. Women are at a disadvantage when it comes to access to information about HIV prevention, the ability to negotiate safe sexual encounters and access to treatment for HIV/AIDS once infected. As a result of those inequities and the dynamics of the epidemic, the proportion of women among people living with HIV/AIDS is rising in many regions.

DISAGGREGATION ISSUES

Data from surveillance of pregnant women at antenatal care clinics are broken into urban populations and populations living outside major urban areas. In many countries, data from rural areas are rare. The indicator for pregnant women ages 15–24 should be reported as the median for the capital city, for other urban areas and for rural areas.

COMMENTS AND LIMITATIONS

The indicator gives a fairly good idea of relatively recent trends in HIV infection nationwide in countries where the epidemic is generalized. In areas where most HIV infections are confined to subpopulations with high-risk behaviours, trends should be assessed in those populations.

In most countries, serosurveillance sites have not been selected as representative samples of the country. Logistical, feasibility and cost issues guide the selection of these sites. In addition, in many countries, the sites included in the surveillance system have changed over time, making interpretation of trends more difficult.

REFERENCES AND INTERNATIONAL DATA COMPARISONS

▶ CAROLINA POPULATION CENTER (2003). *National AIDS Programmes: A Guide to Monitoring and Evaluation*. Chapel Hill. Available from http://www.cpc.unc.edu/ measure/guide/guide.html .

▶ PAN AMERICAN HEALTH ORGANIZATION (2003). *Fact Sheet: Gender and HIV/AIDS*. Washington, D.C. Available from http://www. paho.org/english/hdp/hdw/ GenderandHIVFactSheetI.pdf.

▶ SCHWARTLÄNDER, BERNARD, and OTHERS

(1999). Country-specific estimates and models of HIV and AIDS: methods and limitations. *AIDS*, vol. 13, No. 17.

▶ **UNAIDS** (2002). *Monitoring the Declaration of Commitment on HIV/AIDS: Guidelines on Construction of Core Indicators*. Geneva. Available from http://www.unaids.org/en/ in+ focus/monitoringevaluation.

▶ **UNAIDS** (2003). *Report on the Global HIV/AIDS Epidemic, 2002*, biennial; *AIDS Epidemic Update*. Geneva.

▶ UNITED NATIONS (2003). *Millennium Indicators Database*. Statistics Division Internet site http://millenniumindicators.un.org.

▶ UNITED NATIONS CHILDREN'S FUND (annual). *The State of the World's Children*. New York.

▶ UNITED NATIONS CHILDREN'S FUND, UNAIDS and WORLD HEALTH ORGANIZATION (2002). *Young People and HIV/AIDS: Opportunity in Crisis*. New York.

▶ UNITED NATIONS DEVELOPMENT FUND FOR WOMEN (2000). *Gender, HIV and Human Rights: A Training Manual*. New York. Available from http://www.unifem.undp. org/ resources/hivtraining.

▶ UNITED NATIONS DEVELOPMENT FUND FOR WOMEN (2001). *Turning the Tide: CEDAW and the Gender Dimensions of the HIV/AIDS Pandemic*. New York. Available from http://www. unifem.undp.org/resources/turningtide.

▶ WORLD HEALTH ORGANIZATION (2002). *Second Generation Surveillance for HIV*. Geneva. Available from http://www.who.int/hiv/ pub/surveillance/en.

▶ WORLD HEALTH ORGANIZATION (2002). *Strategic Information*. Geneva. Available from http://www.who.int/hiv/pub/ epdemiology/en.

AGENCIES

Ministries of health
Joint United Nations Programme on HIV/AIDS
World Health Organization
United Nations Children's Fund
United Nations Population Fund

19 CONDOM USE RATE OF THE CONTRACEPTIVE PREVALENCE RATE

DEFINITION
Condom use rate of the contraceptive prevalence rate is the number of women aged 15–49 years in marital or consensual unions who are practising contraception by using condoms as a proportion of all of women of the same age group in consensual unions who are practising, or whose sexual partners are practising, any form of contraception.

GOAL AND TARGET ADDRESSED
Goal 6. Combat HIV/AIDS, malaria and other diseases
Target 7. Have halted by 2015 and begun to reverse the spread of HIV/AIDS

RATIONALE
The condom use rate is used to monitor progress towards halting and reversing the spread of HIV/AIDS, as condoms are the only contraceptive method effective in reducing the spread of HIV. Since the condom use rate is measured only among women in unions, the indicator needs to be supplemented by an indicator on condom use in high-risk situations (see indicator 19a).

METHOD OF COMPUTATION
The number of women ages 15–49 in marital or consensual unions who report that they are using a condom to avoid pregnancy (regardless of whether they are also using additional methods) is divided by the total number of women ages 15–49 in unions who are practising, or whose sexual partners are practising, contraception.

The indicator is not equivalent to condom use prevalence, which is the number of women ages 15–49 in marital or consensual unions who are practising (or whose sexual partners are practising) contraception by using condoms as a percentage of the total number of women of the same age group (and same marital status, if applicable) in the survey.

Irrespective of the contraceptive prevalence rate, if 10 per cent of those practising contraception use condoms, then the rate for indicator 19 is 10 per cent.

The definition and method of calculation of the indicator differ when it is used for monitoring contraceptive use only. In that case, the numerator is the number of women ages 15–49 in marital or consensual unions who report that they are using a condom as their main method of contraception.

DATA COLLECTION AND SOURCE
Contraceptive prevalence data are obtained mainly from household surveys, notably the Demographic and Health Surveys, Multiple Indicator Cluster Surveys and contraceptive prevalence surveys. For condom-use data, married women are asked whether they have ever heard of condoms and then whether they are currently using condoms to prevent pregnancy.

PERIODICITY OF MEASUREMENT
Household surveys, such as Demographic and Health Surveys, Multiple Indicator Cluster Surveys and contraceptive prevalence surveys, are generally conducted every three to five years.

GENDER ISSUES
Statistics on contraception prevalence rates are based primarily on women, mainly because contraception is more easily measured in this way. Further, contraception, or its absence, affects the health and well-being of women more than it does their sexual partners. Similarly, condom use is still at the discretion of male partners, and the female condom is not as widely available. The rising number of women and girls infected by HIV/AIDS indicates that condom use needs further promotion and that women need to be empowered to refuse unprotected sex.

DISAGGREGATION ISSUES
Condom use, as it is the case in general for

contraceptive use, may vary significantly across socio-economic groups and regional and geographical areas. It is important that the analysis address specific demographic groups, such as adolescents and unmarried women.

COMMENTS AND LIMITATIONS

The indicator does not reflect condom use for the unmarried population and people in groups with high-risk behaviour. Data are generally collected for women in consensual unions and in a particular age range, while the population of concern includes all women of reproductive age, irrespective of marital status.

The spread of HIV through sexual relations depends on having unprotected sex with people who also have other partners. Most monogamous relationships are cohabiting, although the reverse is not necessarily true. Partners who do not live together and who have sex only occasionally are most likely to have other partners over the course of a year. These partnerships therefore carry a higher risk of HIV transmission than partnerships that do not link into a wider sexual network. AIDS prevention programmes try to discourage high numbers of partnerships and to encourage mutual monogamy.

Indicator 19, therefore, is not a practical indicator for measuring the prevention of HIV/AIDS. Information should be collected on additional indicators on condom use in high-risk situations (indicator 19A) and on knowledge and misconceptions of HIV/AIDS among 15-24 year-olds (indicator 19B). Such indicators give a better picture of the proportion of the population that engages in relatively high-risk partnerships and that is therefore more likely to be exposed to the sexual networks within which HIV can circulate.

REFERENCES AND INTERNATIONAL DATA COMPARISONS

▸ **ORC Macro** (2003). *Demographic and Health Surveys – Providing Information for Informed Decisions in Population, Health and Nutrition*. Internet site http://www. measuredhs.com. Calverton, Maryland.
▸ **UNAIDS** (2003). Internet site http://www. unaids.org. Geneva.
▸ **United Nations** (1958). *Multilingual Demographic Dictionary*. Population Studies, No. 29. Sales No. E.58.XIII.4.
▸ **United Nations** (2001). *Indicators of Sustainable Development: Guidelines and Methodologies*. Sales No. E.01.II.A.6. Available from http://www.un.org/esa/ sustdev/natlinfo/indicators/isd.htm.
▸ **United Nations** (2001). *Levels and Trends of Contraceptive Use as Assessed in 1998*. Sales No. E.01.XIII.4. Available from http://www.un.org/esa/population/unpop. htm.
▸ **United Nations** (2003). *Millennium Indicators Database*. Statistics Division Internet site http://millenniumindicators.un.org.
▸ **United Nations Children's Fund** (2003). *Progress since the World Summit for Children*. New York. Available from http:// www.childinfo.org; in Quick Access under "Contraceptive prevalence".
▸ **United Nations Children's Fund** (annual). *The State of the World's Children*. New York.
▸ **United Nations Development Fund for Women** (2000). *Gender, HIV and Human Rights: A Training Manual*. New York. Available from http://www.unifem.undp. org/ resources/hivtraining.
▸ **United Nations Development Programme** (2003 and annual). *Human Development Report*. New York: Oxford University Press. Available from http://hdr.undp.org.
▸ **World Bank** (2003 and annual). *World Development Indicators*. Print and CD-ROM. Washington, D.C. Available in part from http://www.worldbank.org/data.
▸ **World Health Organization** (2002 and annual). *World Health Report*. Geneva. Available from http://www.who.int/whr/ en.

AGENCIES

Ministries of health
Joint United Nations Programme on HIV/AIDS
United Nations Children's Fund

United Nations Population Division
World Health Organization
United Nations Population Fund

19.A CONDOM USE AT LAST HIGH-RISK SEX

DEFINITION
Condom use at last high-risk sex is the percentage of young people ages 15–24 reporting the use of a condom during sexual intercourse with a non-regular sexual partner in the last 12 months.

GOAL AND TARGET ADDRESSED
Goal 6. Combat HIV/AIDS, malaria and other diseases
Target 7. Have halted by 2015 and begun to reverse the spread of HIV/AIDS

RATIONALE
Consistent use of condoms in non-regular sexual partnerships substantially reduces the risk of sexual HIV transmission. This is especially important for young people, who often experience the highest rates of HIV infection because they have low prior exposure to infection and (typically) relatively high numbers of non-regular sexual partnerships. Consistent condom use with non-regular sexual partners is important even in countries where HIV prevalence is low because it can prevent the spread of HIV in circumstances where non-regular relationships are common. Condom use is one measure of protection against HIV/AIDS. Equally important are delaying age at first sex, reducing the number of non-regular sexual partners and being faithful to one partner.

METHOD OF COMPUTATION
The number of respondents ages 15–24 who reported having had a non-regular (non-marital and non-cohabiting) sexual partner in the last 12 months and using a condom the last time they had sex with this partner, as a share of the number of respondents ages 15–24 who reported having had a non-regular sexual partner in the last 12 months.

PERIODICITY OF MEASUREMENT
Household surveys, such as Demographic and Health Surveys, rural household surveys and behavioural surveillance surveys, are generally conducted every three to five years.

GENDER ISSUES
Women's risk of becoming infected with HIV during unprotected sexual intercourse is higher than that of men. And the risk is even higher for younger women. Social and cultural factors may increase women's vulnerability to HIV infection. For instance, cultural norms related to sexuality often prevent girls from taking active steps to protect themselves.

COMMENTS AND LIMITATIONS
A rise in the indicator is an extremely powerful sign that condom promotion campaigns are having the desired effect among their principle target market. However, condom promotion campaigns aim for consistent use of condoms with non-regular partners rather than simply occasional use.

Some surveys have tried to ask directly about consistent use, but the question is subject to recall bias and other biases.

The current indicator is therefore considered adequate to address the target since it is assumed that if consistent use rises, use at last high-risk sex will also increase.

DATA COLLECTION AND SOURCE
Data on condom use with non-regular sexual partners are available from household surveys (such as Demographic and Health Surveys, rural household surveys and behavioural surveillance surveys) that collect information on sexual behaviour.

REFERENCES AND INTERNATIONAL DATA COMPARISONS

▶ CAROLINA POPULATION CENTER (2003). *National AIDS Programmes: A Guide to Monitoring and Evaluation.* Chapel Hill. Available from http://www.cpc.unc.edu/measure/guide/guide.html.

▶ UNAIDS (2002). *Monitoring the Declaration of Commitment on HIV/AIDS: Guidelines on Construction of Core Indicators.* Geneva. Available from http://www.unaids.org/en/in+ focus/monitoringevaluation.

▶ UNITED NATIONS CHILDREN'S FUND (annual). *The State of the World's Children.* New York.

▶ UNITED NATIONS CHILDREN'S FUND, UNAIDS and WORLD HEALTH ORGANIZATION (2002). *Young People and HIV/AIDS: Opportunity in Crisis.* New York.

▶ WORLD HEALTH ORGANIZATION, JOINT UNITED NATIONS PROGRAMME ON HIV/AIDS and the UNITED NATIONS CHILDREN'S FUND (2002). *Epidemiological Fact Sheets.* Geneva. Available from http://www.who.int/emc-hiv/fact_sheets.

AGENCIES

Ministries of health
United Nations Children's Fund
United Nations Population Fund

19·B PERCENTAGE OF POPULATION AGED 15–24 YEARS WITH COMPREHENSIVE CORRECT KNOWLEDGE OF HIV/AIDS

DEFINITION

Percentage of population aged 15–24 years with comprehensive correct knowledge of HIV/AIDS is the share of women and men aged 15–24 years who correctly identify the two major ways of preventing the sexual transmission of HIV (using condoms and limiting sex to one faithful, uninfected partner), who reject the two most common local misconceptions about HIV transmission and who know that a healthy-looking person can transmit HIV.

GOAL AND TARGET ADDRESSED

Goal 6. Combat HIV/AIDS, malaria and other diseases
Target 7. Have halted by 2015 and begun to reverse the spread of HIV/AIDS

RATIONALE

The indicator reflects the success of national information, education and communication programmes and other efforts in promoting knowledge of valid HIV-prevention methods and reducing misconceptions about the disease. Common local misconceptions can be determined by the context of the country.

METHOD OF COMPUTATION

Since there are not enough surveys to calculate the indicator as defined above, the United Nations Children's Fund, in collaboration with the Joint United Nations Programme on HIV/AIDS and the World Health Organization, has produced two proxy indicators that represent two components of the actual indicator:

▶ Percentage of women and men ages 15–24 who know that a person can protect him or herself from HIV infection by "consistent use of condom". The indicator is calculated as the number of respondents ages 15–24 who, in response to prompting, correctly identify consistent use of condoms as a means of protection against HIV infection, as a percentage of the total number of respondents ages 15–24.

▶ Percentage of women and men ages 15–24 who know a healthy-looking person can transmit HIV. The indicator is calculated as the number of respondents ages 15–24 who, in response to prompting, correctly note that a person who looks healthy may transmit HIV, as a percentage of the total number of respondents ages 15–24.

DATA COLLECTION AND SOURCE

Data on knowledge of and misconceptions about HIV/AIDS are collected through household surveys (such as Demographic and Health Surveys, rural household surveys, behavioural surveillance surveys and Multiple Indicator Cluster Surveys).

PERIODICITY OF MEASUREMENT

Household surveys, such as Demographic and Health Surveys, rural household surveys, behavioural surveillance surveys and Multiple Indicator Cluster Surveys, are generally conducted every three to five years.

GENDER ISSUES

Women's risk of becoming infected with HIV during unprotected sexual intercourse is higher than that of men. The risk is even higher for younger women. Social and cultural factors may increase women's vulnerability to HIV infection. For instance, cultural norms related to sexuality often prevent girls from taking active steps to protect themselves.

In many countries, girls are becoming infected and dying younger than boys, for various reasons, especially in sub-Saharan Africa, the region most affected by HIV/AIDS.

COMMENTS AND LIMITATIONS:

See "Methods of computation".

REFERENCES AND INTERNATIONAL DATA COMPARISONS

- ▸ CAROLINA POPULATION CENTER (2003). *National AIDS Programmes: A Guide to Monitoring and Evaluation*. Chapel Hill. Available from http://www.cpc.unc.edu/measure/guide/guide.html.
- ▸ ORC MACRO (2003). *Demographic and Health Surveys – Providing Information for Informed Decisions in Population, Health and Nutrition*. Internet site http://www.measuredhs.com. Calverton, USA.
- ▸ UNAIDS (2002). *Monitoring the Declaration of Commitment on HIV/AIDS: Guidelines on Construction of Core Indicators*. Geneva.

Available from http://www.unaids.org/en/in+focus/monitoringevaluation. Select: Guidelines on construction of core indicators.

- ▸ UNITED NATIONS CHILDREN'S FUND (annual). *The State of the World's Children*. New York.
- ▸ UNITED NATIONS CHILDREN'S FUND, UNAIDS and WORLD HEALTH ORGANIZATION (2002). *Young People and HIV/AIDS: Opportunity in Crisis*. New York.
- ▸ WORLD HEALTH ORGANIZATION, JOINT UN PROGRAMME ON HIV/AIDS and the UNITED NATIONS CHILDREN'S FUND (2002). *Epidemiological Fact Sheets*. Geneva. Available from http://www.who.int/emc-hiv/ fact_sheets.

AGENCY

United Nations Children's Fund.

CONTRACEPTIVE PREVALENCE RATE

DEFINITION

The *contraceptive prevalence rate* is the percentage of women who are practising, or whose sexual partners are practising, any form of contraception. It is usually reported for women ages 15–49 in marital or consensual unions.

GOAL AND TARGET ADDRESSED

Goal 6. Combat HIV/AIDS, malaria and other diseases

Target 7. Have halted by 2015 and begun to reverse the spread of HIV/AIDS

RATIONALE

The indicator is useful in tracking progress towards health, gender and poverty goals. It also serves as a proxy measure of access to reproductive health services that are essential for meeting many of the goals, especially the child and maternity mortality and HIV/AIDS goals.

Contraceptive methods include condoms, female and male sterilization, injectable and oral hormones, intrauterine devices, diaphragms, spermicides and natural family planning, as well as lactational amenorrhoea (lack of menstruation during breastfeeding) where it is cited as a method. Since, among contraceptive methods, only condoms are effective in preventing HIV infections, specific indicators on condom use are also considered (SEE INDICATORS 19, 19A and 19B).

METHOD OF COMPUTATION
The number of women ages 15–49 in marital or consensual unions who report that they are practising (or whose sexual partners are practising) contraception is divided by the total number of women ages 15–49 (and same marital status, if applicable) in the survey.

DATA COLLECTION AND SOURCE
Contraceptive prevalence data are obtained mainly from household surveys, notably the Demographic and Health Surveys, Multiple Indicator Cluster Surveys and contraceptive prevalence surveys.

PERIODICITY OF MEASUREMENT
Household surveys, such as Demographic and Health Surveys, Multiple Indicator Cluster Surveys and contraceptive prevalence surveys, are generally conducted every three to five years.

GENDER ISSUES
Statistics on contraception prevalence rates are based primarily on women, mainly because contraception is more easily measured in this way. Further, contraception, or its absence, affects the health and well-being of women more than it does their sexual partners.

DISAGGREGATION ISSUES
Contraceptive use may vary significantly across socio-economic groups and regional and geographical areas. It is important that the analysis address specific demographic groups, such as adolescents and unmarried women.

COMMENTS AND LIMITATIONS
Data are generally collected for women in unions and in a particular age range, while the population of concern includes all women of reproductive age, irrespective of marital status.

In addition, contraceptive methods may include traditional methods that are largely ineffective. It is important, to the extent possible, to at least distinguish between traditional and modern methods.

Underreporting can occur when the interviewer does not mention specific methods, such as contraceptive surgical sterilization.

REFERENCES AND INTERNATIONAL DATA COMPARISONS
- **ORC MACRO** (2003). *Demographic and Health Surveys–Providing Information for Informed Decisions in Population, Health and Nutrition*. Internet site http://www.measuredhs.com. Calverton, Maryland.
- **UNITED NATIONS** (1958). *Multilingual Demographic Dictionary, English Section*, Population Studies, No. 29. Sales No. E.58.XIII.4.
- **UNITED NATIONS** (2001). *Indicators of Sustainable Development: Guidelines and Methodologies*. Sales No. E.01.II.A.6. Available from: http://www.un.org/esa/sustdev/natlinfo/indicators/isd.htm.
- **UNITED NATIONS** (2001). *Levels and Trends of Contraceptive Use as Assessed in 1998*. Sales No. E.01.XIII.4. Available from http://www.un.org/esa/population/unpop.htm.
- **UNITED NATIONS** (2002). *World Contraceptive Use 2001*. Wall Chart. Sales No. E.02.XIII.7. Available from http://www.un.org/esa/population/publications/contraceptive2001/contraception01.htm.
- **UNITED NATIONS CHILDREN'S FUND** (annual). *The State of the World's Children*. New York.
- **UNITED NATIONS DEVELOPMENT FUND FOR WOMEN** (2000). *Gender, HIV and Human Rights: A Training Manual*. New York. Available from

http://www.unifem.undp.org/resources/ hivtraining .

▶ **UNITED NATIONS DEVELOPMENT PROGRAMME** (2003 and annual). *Human Development Report*. New York: Oxford University Press. Available from http://hdr.undp.org.

▶ **UNITED NATIONS POPULATION FUND** (annual). *State of World Population*. Available from http://www.unfpa.org/swp/swpmain.htm.

▶ **WORLD BANK** (2003 and annual). *World Development Indicators*. Print and CD-ROM. Washington, D.C. Available in part from http://www.worldbank.org/data.

▶ **WORLD HEALTH ORGANIZATION** (2002 and annual). *World Health Report*. Geneva. Available from http://www.who.int/whr/ en.

AGENCIES
Ministry of health
United Nations Population Fund
United Nations Children's Fund
United Nations Population Division

20 RATIO OF SCHOOL ATTENDANCE OF ORPHANS TO SCHOOL ATTENDANCE OF NON-ORPHANS AGED 10–14 YEARS

DEFINITION
Strictly defined, the number of children orphaned by HIV/AIDS is the estimated number of children who have lost their mother, father or both parents to AIDS before age 15. In practice, the impact of the AIDS epidemic on orphans is measured through the ratio of orphans to non-orphans who are in school.

GOAL AND TARGET ADDRESSED
Goal 6. Combat HIV/AIDS, malaria and other diseases
Target 7. Have halted by 2015 and begun to reverse the spread of HIV/AIDS

RATIONALE
HIV/AIDS is claiming the lives of ever-growing numbers of adults just when they are forming families and bringing up children. As a result, orphan prevalence is rising steadily in many countries, while fewer relatives within the prime adult ages mean that orphaned children face an increasingly uncertain future.

Orphanhood is frequently accompanied by prejudice and increased poverty—factors that can further jeopardize children's well-being. Children and adolescents orphaned by AIDS face decreased access to adequate nutrition, basic health care, housing and clothing. They may turn to survival strategies that increase their vulnerability to HIV. They are likely to drop out of school owing to discrimination, emotional distress, inability to pay school fees or the need to care for parents or caretakers infected with HIV or for younger siblings. In sub-Saharan Africa, only 60 per cent of orphans (ages 10–14) who lost both parents attend school as compared with 71 per cent of those with both parents still living. The limited countries with trend data indicate a widening of the gap. It is important, therefore, to monitor the extent to which AIDS support programmes succeed in securing educational opportunities for orphaned children.

METHOD OF COMPUTATION
The current school attendance rate of children ages 10–14 for whom both biological parents have died is divided by the current school attendance rate of children ages 10–14 whose parents are both still alive and who live with at least one biological parent.

DATA COLLECTION AND SOURCE
Data for the indicator are collected through household surveys (such as Demographic and Health Surveys and Multiple Indicator Cluster Surveys).

PERIODICITY OF MEASUREMENT
Household surveys, such as Demographic and Health Surveys and Multiple Indicator Cluster Surveys, are generally conducted every three to five years.

GENDER ISSUES

Boys and girls are both affected. However, girls might be more likely than boys to leave school to care for ill parents and younger siblings.

DISAGGREGATION ISSUES

Data should be presented separately for boys and girls.

COMMENTS AND LIMITATIONS

The indicator is confined to children ages 10–14 for comparability, as age at school entry varies across countries. Household surveys can miss children in unstable households, and orphaned children are disproportionately likely to be in such households.

The indicator is not a direct measure of the number of children orphaned by HIV/AIDS, despite the wording. The indicator does not directly distinguish the cause of orphanhood. However, it is believed that high proportions of deaths of adults with school-age children in areas of HIV epidemics are likely to be related to HIV/AIDS.

REFERENCES AND INTERNATIONAL DATA COMPARISONS

▸ CAROLINA POPULATION CENTER (2003). *National AIDS Programmes: A Guide to Monitoring and Evaluation*. Chapel Hill. Available from http://www.cpc.unc.edu/measure/guide/guide.html.

▸ UNAIDS (2002). *Monitoring the Declaration of Commitment on HIV/AIDS: Guidelines on Construction of Core Indicators*. Geneva. Available from http://www.unaids.org/en/in+ focus/monitoringevaluation.

▸ UNITED NATIONS (1998). *Principles and Recommendations for Population and Housing Censuses, Revision 1*, Series M, No. 67, Rev. 1. Sales No. E.98.XVII.1. Available from http://unstats. un.org/unsd/pubs (A, E, F, S).

▸ UNITED NATIONS CHILDREN'S FUND (annual). *The State of the World's Children*. New York.

▸ UNITED NATIONS CHILDREN'S FUND, UNAIDS and UNITED STATES AGENCY FOR INTERNATIONAL DEVELOPMENT (2002). *Children on the Brink 2002: A Joint Report on Orphan Estimates and Program Strategies*.

▸ UNITED NATIONS CHILDREN'S FUND, UNAIDS and WORLD HEALTH ORGANIZATION (2002). *Young People and HIV/AIDS: Opportunity in Crisis*. New York.

AGENCIES

Joint United Nations Programme on HIV/AIDS
United Nations Children's Fund

21 PREVALENCE AND DEATH RATES ASSOCIATED WITH MALARIA

DEFINITION

Prevalence of malaria is the number of cases of malaria per 100,000 people. *Death rates associated with malaria* refers to the number of deaths caused by malaria per 100,000 people.

GOAL AND TARGET ADDRESSED

Goal 6. Combat HIV/AIDS, malaria and other diseases

Target 8. Have halted by 2015 and begun to reverse the incidence of malaria and other major diseases

RATIONALE

The indicator allows highly endemic countries to monitor disease and death from malaria, which have been increasing over the last two decades owing to deteriorating health systems, growing drug and insecticide resistance, periodic changes in weather patterns, civil unrest, human migration and population displacement.

METHOD OF COMPUTATION

Where the only prevalence data available are reported through the administration of health services, they are expressed per 100,000 population, using population estimates as the denominator.

Where prevalence data on children under five come from household surveys, the data may be reported as percentages of children under five with fever in the last two weeks. The percentage may be multiplied by 1,000 to express the rate per 100,000.

The World Health Organization also produces model-based estimates of malaria-specific mortality.

DATA COLLECTION AND SOURCE

Data come from administrative sources, household surveys and vital statistics registrations. Administrative data are derived by health ministries from the administration of health services. Multiple Indicator Cluster Surveys collect information on the prevalence of fever in the last two weeks for children under five. The surveys also provide data on all causes of under-five mortality.

Vital statistics registration systems collect data on cause of death, including deaths caused by malaria. Good quality information requires that death registration be near universal, that the cause of death be reported routinely on the death record and that it be determined by a qualified observer according to the International Classification of Diseases. Such information is not generally available in developing countries but is now compiled by WHO annually for approximately 70 (mainly developed) countries.

PERIODICITY OF MEASUREMENT

Administrative data are, in principle, available annually. Data from surveys are generally available every three to five years.

GENDER ISSUES

Potential differences between men and women are a function of the interaction between biological factors and gender roles and relations. Biological factors vary between men and women and influence susceptibility and immunity to tropical diseases. Gender roles and relations influence the degree of exposure to the relevant vectors and also to the access and control of resources needed to protect women and men from being infected. Women's immunity is particularly compromised during pregnancy, making pregnant women more likely to become infected and implying differential severity of the consequences. Malaria during pregnancy is an important cause of maternal mortality.

DISAGGREGATION ISSUES

All data should be classified by sex, as there could be differential death rates.

Rural populations carry the overwhelming burden of disease, so urban and rural disaggregation of the data is important in tracking the progress made in rural areas. Multiple Indicator Cluster Surveys data have shown substantial difference by wealth quintiles, and where possible the data should be disaggregated by a wealth index.

COMMENTS AND LIMITATIONS

Malaria statistics are reported in countries where it is endemic, which includes almost all developing countries. However, data reported by ministries are often only a fraction of the number of cases in the population. Many report only laboratory-confirmed cases. In sub-Saharan Africa, clinically diagnosed cases also tend to be reported.

Differences between male and female prevalence and incidence rates are difficult to measure since malaria in women is more likely to be undetected. The fact that health services focus almost exclusively on women's reproductive function means that opportunities are lost for detection of multiple conditions, including tropical diseases. Moreover, when incidence rates in women and men are similar, there are still significant differences between them in the susceptibility and the impact of tropical diseases.

REFERENCES AND INTERNATIONAL DATA

COMPARISONS

▸ GUNN, S.W.A., KLUWER ACADEMIC PUBLISHERS (1990). *Multilingual Dictionary of Disaster Medicine and International Relief.* Dordrecht, The Netherlands. English/Français/Español /Arabic.

▸ UNITED NATIONS CHILDREN'S FUND (annual). *The State of the World's Children.* New York.

▸ UNITED NATIONS DEVELOPMENT PROGRAMME (2003 and annual). *Human Development Report.* New York: Oxford University Press. Available from http://hdr.undp.org.

▸ WORLD BANK (2003 and annual). *World Development Indicators.* Print and CD-ROM. Washington, D.C. Available in part from http://www.worldbank.org/data.

▸ WORLD BANK, UNITED NATIONS CHILDREN'S FUND, WORLD HEALTH ORGANIZATION and UNITED NATIONS DEVELOPMENT PROGRAMME (2003). *Roll Back Malaria (RBM). A Global Partnership.* Internet site http://www.rbm. who.int/. Geneva.

▸ WORLD HEALTH ORGANIZATION (1992). *International Statistical Classification of Diseases and Related Health Problems, Tenth Revision (ICD-10),* vol. 1. Geneva.

▸ WORLD HEALTH ORGANIZATION (1998). *Gender and Health: Technical Paper.* WHO/FRH/WHD/98.16. Geneva. Available from http://www.who.int/reproductive-health/publications. Select: Gender.

▸ WORLD HEALTH ORGANIZATION (2002 and annual). *World Health Report.* Geneva. Available from http://www.who.int/whr/ en.

▸ WORLD HEALTH ORGANIZATION (2002). *2001-2010: United Nations Decade to Roll Back Malaria: Monitoring and Evaluation.* Geneva. Available from http://www.who. int/inf-fs/en/informationSheet11.pdf.

▸ WORLD HEALTH ORGANIZATION (2003). *WHO Statistical Information System (WHOSIS)— Evidence and Information for Health Policy.* Internet site http://www3.who.int/whosis/ menu.cfm. Geneva.

▸ WORLD HEALTH ORGANIZATION and UNITED NATIONS CHILDREN'S FUND (2003). *Africa*

Malaria Report. Available from http://www. rbm.who.int/amd2003/amr2003/ amr_toc.htm .

AGENCIES
Ministries of health
United Nations Children's Fund
World Health Organization

22 PROPORTION OF POPULATION IN MALARIA-RISK AREAS USING EFFECTIVE MALARIA PREVENTION AND TREATMENT MEASURES

DEFINITION

Malaria prevention is measured as the percentage of children ages 0–59 months sleeping under insecticide-treated bednets. *Malaria treatment* among children is measured as the proportion of children ages 0–59 months who were ill with fever in the two weeks before the survey and who received appropriate antimalarial drugs.

GOAL AND TARGET ADDRESSED

Goal 6. Combat HIV/AIDS, malaria and other diseases

Target 8. Have halted by 2015 and begun to reverse the incidence of malaria and other major diseases

RATIONALE

The Roll Back Malaria initiative, established in late 1998 by the World Health Organization, the United Nations Children's Fund and the World Bank, identifies four main interventions to reduce the burden of malaria in Africa:

■ Use of insecticide-treated bednets, which have been demonstrated to cut all-cause child mortality over the first two years by 20 per cent.

■ Prompt access to effective treatment in or near the home.

■ Provision of antimalarial drugs to symptom-free pregnant women in high transmission areas.

■ Improved forecasting, prevention and rapid response to malaria epidemics.

In areas of sub-Saharan Africa with high levels of malaria transmission, regular use of an insecticide-treated bednet can reduce mortality in children under five years of age by as much as 20 per cent and has a significant impact on anemia. Similar or greater benefits have been achieved in other regions and for pregnant women. The prevention indicator will allow countries to monitor widespread use of insecticide-treated materials and other appropriate methods to limit contact between humans and mosquitoes.

Detection of epidemics requires timely, complete surveillance of malaria cases and monitoring of weather patterns. Reserve drug stocks, transport and hospital capacity are needed to mount an appropriate response. In some epidemic zones, well-timed and targeted vector control activities have minimized the impact of epidemics. The treatment indicator allows countries to monitor detection and appropriate response to epidemics within two weeks of onset.

METHOD OF COMPUTATION
For prevention, the indicator is calculated as the percentage of children under five years of age in the survey who slept under an insecticide-treated bednet the previous night.

DATA COLLECTION AND SOURCE
The only data sources are household surveys, mainly Demographic and Health Surveys and the Multiple Indicator Cluster Surveys, malaria surveys and malaria modules added to other ongoing household surveys.

PERIODICITY OF MEASUREMENT
Data on coverage of insecticide-treated bednets and treatment data should be collected about every two to three years.

GENDER ISSUES
Girls may have greater exposure than boys to malaria-infested areas owing to their role in the provision of fuel, water and other supplies.

DISAGGREGATION ISSUES
Disparities by sex, age, mother's education and area of residence should be assessed.

COMMENTS AND LIMITATIONS
Survey data are subject to sampling errors and are undertaken only every few years. As the data on bednet use are new, no trend data are yet available.

REFERENCES AND INTERNATIONAL DATA COMPARISONS

▶ GUNN, S.W.A. (1990). *Multilingual Dictionary of Disaster Medicine and International Relief*. Dordrecht, The Netherlands: KLUWER ACADEMIC PUBLISHERS. English/Français/Español/Arabic.

▶ UNITED NATIONS CHILDREN'S FUND (2003). The Challenge – Scope of the Problem. Internet site http://www.childinfo.org/eddb/Malaria. New York.

▶ UNITED NATIONS CHILDREN'S FUND (annual). *The State of the World's Children*. New York.

▶ UNITED NATIONS DEVELOPMENT PROGRAMME (2003 and annual). *Human Development Report*. New York: Oxford University Press. Available from http://hdr.undp.org.

▶ WORLD BANK, UNITED NATIONS CHILDREN'S FUND, WORLD HEALTH ORGANIZATION and UNITED NATIONS DEVELOPMENT PROGRAMME (2003). *Roll Back Malaria - A Global Partnership*. Internet site http://www.rbm.who.int. Geneva.

▶ WORLD HEALTH ORGANIZATION (2002). *2001-2010: United Nations Decade to Roll Back Malaria: Monitoring and evaluation*. Geneva. Available from http://www.who.int/ inf-fs/en/informationSheet11.pdf.

▶ WORLD HEALTH ORGANIZATION (2002 and annual). *World Health Report*. Geneva. Available from http://www.who.int/whr/en.

AGENCIES
Ministries of health
United Nations Children's Fund
World Health Organization

23 PREVALENCE AND DEATH RATES ASSOCIATED WITH TUBERCULOSIS

DEFINITION

Tuberculosis prevalence is the number of cases of tuberculosis per 100,000 people. *Death rates associated with tuberculosis* refers to the number of deaths caused by tuberculosis per 100,000 people. A *tuberculosis case* is defined as a patient in whom tuberculosis has been bacteriologically confirmed or diagnosed by a clinician.

GOAL AND TARGET ADDRESSED

Goal 6. Combat HIV/AIDS, malaria and other diseases
Target 8. Have halted by 2015 and begun to reverse the incidence of malaria and other major diseases

RATIONALE

Detecting tuberculosis and curing it are key interventions for addressing poverty and inequality. Prevalence and deaths are more sensitive markers of the changing burden of tuberculosis than incidence (new cases), although data on trends in incidence are far more comprehensive and give the best overview of the impact of global tuberculosis control.

METHOD OF COMPUTATION

Where the only data available are data reported through the administration of health services, they are expressed per 100,000 population, using population estimates as the denominator.

Where the data come from household surveys, prevalence (and more rarely deaths) is expressed per 100,000 population, using the total population in the survey as the denominator.

Tuberculosis prevalence is sometimes expressed in absolute numbers of cases, while tuberculosis incidence in a given period (usually one year) is always per 100,000 people.

DATA COLLECTION AND SOURCE

Direct measures of tuberculosis prevalence are uncommon, and recent population-based surveys have been confined largely to countries in East Asia and the Pacific . Direct measures of the tuberculosis death rate come from vital statistics registration. Reliable figures require that death registration be nearly universal and that the cause of death be reported routinely on the death record and determined by a qualified observer according to the International Classification of Diseases. Such information is not generally available in developing countries. Vital statistics registration systems tend to underestimate tuberculosis deaths, although time series data from some countries in Asia and the Americas give a useful indication of trends.

In the absence of direct measures of prevalence and death rates, a variety of techniques can be used to estimate these values. Administrative data are derived from the administration of health services. Data can also be obtained from such household surveys as Multiple Indicator Cluster Surveys or the Demographic and Health Surveys, although they usually refer only to children under five and do not provide death rates. Population data come directly or indirectly from population censuses.

PERIODICITY OF MEASUREMENT

Administrative data are, in principle, available annually. Data from surveys are generally available every three to five years. Results from population censuses are generally available every 10 years.

GENDER ISSUES

At younger ages, the prevalence of infection is similar in boys and girls. At older ages, a higher prevalence has been found in men; in most of the world, more men than women are diagnosed with tuberculosis and die from it. However, recent analyses comparing infection and disease rates suggest that the propensity to develop the disease after infection with mycobacterium tuberculosis (the progression rate) may be greater among women of reproductive age than among men of the same age. A recent review of socio-economic and cultural factors relating to the suggested differences called for further research to clarify such differences in the epidemiology of tuberculosis.

Although more men than women die of tuberculosis, it is still a leading cause of death from infectious disease among women. Since tuberculosis affects women mainly in their economically and reproductively active years, the impact of the disease is also strongly felt by their children and families.

DISAGGREGATION ISSUES
It is important to compile data by sex and to take a gender perspective in the analysis.

COMMENTS AND LIMITATIONS
Tuberculosis prevalence and death rate data reported by ministries in developing countries are usually only a fraction of the number of cases and deaths from tuberculosis in the population.

REFERENCES AND INTERNATIONAL DATA COMPARISONS
▸ GUNN, S.W.A. (1990). *Multilingual Dictionary of Disaster Medicine and International Relief*. Dordrecht, The Netherlands: **Kluwer Academic Publishers** . English/Français/Español/Arabic.
▸ UNITED NATIONS DEVELOPMENT PROGRAMME (2003 and annual). *Human Development Report*. New York: Oxford University Press. Available from http://hdr.undp.org.
▸ WORLD BANK (2003 and annual). *World Development Indicators*. Print and CD-ROM. Washington, D.C. Available in part from http://www.worldbank.org/data.
▸ WORLD HEALTH ORGANIZATION (1992).

International Statistical Classification of Diseases and Related Health Problems, Tenth Revision (ICD-10), vol. 1. Geneva.
▸ WORLD HEALTH ORGANIZATION (1998). Gender and Health, Technical Paper. Geneva. Available from http://www.who.int/reproductive-health/publications.
▸ WORLD HEALTH ORGANIZATION (2002 and annual). *World Health Report*. Geneva. Available from http://www.who.int/whr/en.
▸ WORLD HEALTH ORGANIZATION (2003). *Global Tuberculosis Control – Surveillance, Planning, Financing*. WHO Report 2003. Geneva.
▸ WORLD HEALTH ORGANIZATION (2003). *WHO Statistical Information System (WHOSIS)— Evidence and Information for Health Policy*. Internet site http://www3.who.int/whosis/menu.cfm. Geneva.

AGENCIES
Ministries of health.
World Health Organization.

24 PROPORTION OF TUBERCULOSIS CASES DETECTED AND CURED UNDER INTERNATIONALLY RECOMMENDED TB CONTROL STRATEGY

DEFINITION
The *tuberculosis detection* rate is the percentage of estimated new infectious tuberculosis cases detected under the internationally recommended tuberculosis control strategy DOTS. DOTS combines five elements—political commitment, microscopy services, drug supplies, surveillance and monitoring systems and use of highly efficacious regimes—with direct observation of treatment. The *cure rate* is the percentage of new, registered smear-positive (infectious) cases that were cured or in which a full course of DOTS was completed. A *tuberculosis case* is defined as a patient in whom tuberculosis has been bateriologically confirmed or diagnosed by a clinician.

GOAL AND TARGET ADDRESSED

Goal 6. Combat HIV/AIDS, malaria and other diseases

Target 8. Have halted by 2015 and begun to reverse the incidence of malaria and other major diseases

RATIONALE

Since tuberculosis is an airborne contagious disease, primary control is effected through finding and treating infectious cases and thus limiting the risk of acquiring infection. The recommended approach to primary control is the DOTS strategy, an inexpensive strategy that could prevent millions of tuberculosis cases and deaths over the coming decade.

DOTS is a proven system based on accurate diagnosis and consistent treatment with a full course of a mixture of anti-tuberculosis drugs (isoniazid, rifampicin, pyrazinamide, streptomycin and ethambutol). DOTS requires government commitment, careful detection, consistent treatment, uninterrupted supply of anti-tuberculosis drugs and a monitoring and reporting system to evaluate treatment outcomes for each patient.

METHOD OF COMPUTATION

The case detection rate is the ratio of smear-positive case notifications in a given year to the estimated number of new smear-positive cases arising in that year. For some countries, there is a margin of uncertainty in the estimation of the denominator of this ratio.

The treatment success rates is the ratio of new, registered smear-positive (infectious) cases that were cured or that completed a full course of DOTS to the total number of new, registered cases. Treatment success rates can be monitored directly and accurately in cohorts of patients treated under the DOTS strategy. Systematic evaluation of patient progress and treatment outcomes provides the numerator.

DATA COLLECTION AND SOURCE

Data on both the detection rate and the treatment success rate are derived from World Health Organization DOTS programmes, which monitor and report cases detected, treatment progress and programme performance.

PERIODICITY OF MEASUREMENT

Administrative data are, in principle, available annually. Household surveys are generally available annually. Household surveys are generally available every three to five years. Data from DOTS programmes, though incomplete, are updated frequently.

GENDER ISSUES

At younger ages, the prevalence of infection is similar in boys and girls. At older ages, a higher prevalence has been found in men; in most of the world, more men than women are diagnosed with tuberculosis and die from it. However, recent analyses comparing infection and disease rates suggest that the propensity to develop the disease after infection with mycobacterium tuberculosis (the progression rate) may be greater among women of reproductive age than among men of the same age. A recent review of socio-economic and cultural factors relating to the suggested differences called for further research to clarify such differences in the epidemiology of tuberculosis.

Tuberculosis is nevertheless a leading cause of death from infectious disease among women. Since tuberculosis affects women mainly in their economically and reproductively active years, the impact of the disease is also strongly felt by their children and families.

COMMENTS AND LIMITATIONS

Tuberculosis cases reported by ministries in developing countries are usually only a fraction of the number of cases in the population. It is estimated that in 2000 only 27 per cent of new cases were notified under DOTS and only about 19 per cent of cases were successfully treated.

REFERENCES AND INTERNATIONAL DATA COMPARISONS

▶ GUNN, S.W.A., (1990). *Multilingual Dictionary of Disaster Medicine and International Relief*. Dordrecht, The Netherlands: **Kluwer Academic Publishers**. English/Français/Español/Arabic.

▶ STOP TB PARTNERSHIP (2003). *Stop Tuberculosis, the Stop TB Partnetship*. Internet site http://www.stoptb.org .

▶ WORLD HEALTH ORGANIZATION (1992). *International Statistical Classification of Diseases and Related Health Problems, Tenth Revision (ICD-10)*, vol. 1. Geneva.

▶ WORLD HEALTH ORGANIZATION (2002 and annual). *World Health Report*. Geneva. Available from http://www.who.int/whr/en.

▶ WORLD HEALTH ORGANIZATION (2003). *Global Tuberculosis Control – Surveillance, Planning, Financing. WHO Report 2003*. Geneva.

▶ WORLD HEALTH ORGANIZATION (2003). *WHO Statistical Information System (WHOSIS)— Evidence and Information for Health Policy*. Internet site http://www3.who.int/whosis/menu.cfm. Geneva.

AGENCIES

Ministries of health
World Health Organization

25 PROPORTION OF LAND AREA COVERED BY FOREST

DEFINITION

The Proportion of land area covered by forest is the forest areas as a share of total land area, where *land area* is the total surface area of the country less the area covered by inland waters, such as major rivers and lakes. As defined by the Food and Agriculture Organization of the United Nations in *Global Forest Resources Assessmen, 2000, forest* includes both natural forests and forest plantations. It refers to land with an existing or expected tree canopy of more than 10 per cent and an area of more than 0.5 hectare where the trees should be able to reach a minimum height of five metres. Forests are identified by both the presence of trees and the absence of other land uses. Land from which forest has been cleared but that will be reforested in the foreseeable future is included. Excluded are stands of trees established primarily for agricultural production, such as fruit tree plantations.

GOAL AND TARGET ADDRESSED

Goal 7. Ensure environmental sustainability
Target 9. Integrate the principles of sustainable development into country policies and programmes and reverse the loss of environmental resources

RATIONALE

The indicator provides a measure of the relative importance of a forest in a country. Changes in forest area reflect the demand for land for other competitive uses.

Forests fulfil a number of functions that are vital for humanity, including the provision of goods (timber and non-timber products) and services such as protection against flooding, habitat for biodiversity, carbon sequestration, watershed protection and soil conservation. Large areas of the world's forests have been converted to other uses or severely degraded. While substantial areas of productive forest remain, there is now widespread recognition that the resource is not infinite and that its wise and sustainable use is needed for humanity's survival.

METHOD OF COMPUTATION

The proportion of forest in the total land area is calculated from information provided by countries or from satellite images or other remote sensing information analysis. Changes in the proportion should be computed to identify trends.

DATA COLLECTION AND SOURCE

FAO global forest resource assessments, regional forest resource assessments, special studies and surveys, national forest inventories and satellite images.

PERIODICITY OF MEASUREMENT

FAO global forest resource assessments are carried out every 5–10 years, incorporating national forest resource variables, which are measured in the national forest inventory process at different intervals (often 5–10 years).

GENDER ISSUES

Men and women use forest products in different ways. Women typically gather forest products for fuel, fencing, food for the family, fodder for livestock, medicine and raw materials for income-generating activities. Women are also often the chief sources of information on the use and management of trees and other forest plants. Men, on the other hand, tend to use non-wood forest products, but also more often cut wood to sell or use for building materials. Women's access to forest products may not be ensured—even where women have ownership rights to land.

DISAGGREGATION ISSUES

FAO provides a breakdown of forest cover between natural forest and plantation for developing countries only.

COMMENTS AND LIMITATIONS

National forest inventories and forest surveys are irregular in some countries and may be significantly out of date. Owing to climatic and geographical differences, forest areas vary in importance among countries. Over time, changes in area covered by forests as well as area covered by forests should be documented. Longer time series may be difficult to compare directly without analysis of differences in definitions, methods and underlying data.

The proportion of total forest cover (including both natural forest and plantation) may underestimate the rate at which natural forest is disappearing in some countries.

It is also recommended that immediate users or beneficiaries of wooded land be identified.

REFERENCES AND INTERNATIONAL DATA COMPARISONS

▸ FOOD AND AGRICULTURE ORGANIZATION OF THE UNITED NATIONS (2000). *Global Forest Resources Assessment, 2000*. Rome. Available from http://www.fao.org/forestry/fo/fra.

▸ FOOD AND AGRICULTURE ORGANIZATION OF THE UNITED NATIONS (2003 and biennial). *State of the World's Forests*. Available from http://www.fao.org/DOCREP/005/Y7581E/Y7581E00.HTM.

▸ UNITED NATIONS ECONOMIC COMMISSION FOR EUROPE (2000). *Forest Resources of Europe, CIS, North America, Australia, Japan and New Zealand*. Sales No. 99.II.E.96. Available from http://www.unece.org/ trade/timber/fra/ pdf/contents.htm.

▸ UNITED NATIONS. ECONOMIC COMMISSION FOR EUROPE. CONFERENCE OF EUROPEAN STATISTICS (1989). *ECE Standard Statistical Classification of Land Use*. Geneva. Available from http://www.unescap.org/stat/ envstat/stwes-class-landuse.pdf.

▸ UNITED NATIONS ENVIRONMENT PROGRAMME (2003). Internet site http://www.unep.org. Nairobi.

▸ WORLD BANK (2003 and annual). *World Development Indicators*. Print and CD-ROM. Washington, D.C. Available in part from http:// www.worldbank.org/data.

Although the FAO forestry-related definitions are clear and applied at the international level, countries have historically used their own definitions in conducting national forest inventories and assessments. Considerable efforts have been made to adjust data based on national definitions to comparable international ones, and FAO documents those adjustments in *Global Forest Resources Assessment.*

AGENCIES
Ministries of environment
Food and Agriculture Organization of the United Nations

26 RATIO OF AREA PROTECTED TO MAINTAIN BIOLOGICAL DIVERSITY TO SURFACE AREA

DEFINITION
The *ratio of area protected to maintain biological diversity to surface area* is defined as nationally protected area as a percentage of total surface area of a country. The generally accepted IUCN–World Conservation Union definition of a *protected area* is an area of land or sea dedicated to the protection and maintenance of biological diversity and of natural and associated cultural resources and managed through legal or other effective means.

GOAL AND TARGET ADDRESSED
Goal 7 Ensure environmental sustainability
Target 9. Integrate the principles of sustainable development into country policies and programmes and reverse the loss of environmental resources

RATIONALE
Habitat conservation is vital for stemming the decline in biodiversity. The establishment of protected areas is an important mechanism for achieving that aim. Some areas, such as scientific reserves, are maintained in their natural state and closed to extractive use. Others are partially protected and may be used for recreation or tourism.

In addition to protecting biodiversity, protected areas have become places of high social and economic value: supporting local livelihoods; protecting watersheds from erosion; harbouring an untold wealth of genetic resources; supporting thriving recreation and

tourism industries; providing for science, research and education; and forming a basis for cultural and other non-material values. Those values continue to grow in importance.

METHOD OF COMPUTATION
Protected areas, both terrestrial and marine, are totalled and expressed as a percentage of the total surface area of the country. The total surface area of the country includes terrestrial area plus any territorial sea area (up to 12 nautical miles).

DATA COLLECTION AND SOURCE
Data are collected by ministries of environment and other ministries responsible for the designation and maintenance of protected areas. Data are stored in the World Database on Protected Areas and can be accessed at http://sea.unep-wcmc. org/ wdbpa/UN.cfm.

PERIODICITY OF MEASUREMENT
Data are constantly updated in the World Database on Protected Areas as new information is received from countries.

GENDER ISSUES
Mainstream agricultural, environmental and related policies and programmes tend to envision farmers as men and often fail to recognize women's work, knowledge, contributions and needs. This tendency has important consequences for biodiversity as well as for gender equality.

COMMENTS AND LIMITATIONS
The designation of an area as protected is not confirmation that protection measures are actually in force. The indicator provides a measure of Governments' will to protect biodiversity. It does not measure the effectiveness of policy tools in reducing biodiversity loss, which ultimately depends on a range of management and implementation factors not covered by the indicator.

The indicator provides no information on areas

that are not designated as protected but that may also be important for conserving biodiversity.

The data also do not include sites protected under local or provincial law.

No quantified target has been established for this indicator.

REFERENCES AND INTERNATIONAL DATA COMPARISONS

▸ ORGANISATION FOR ECONOMIC CO-OPERATION AND DEVELOPMENT/DEVELOPMENT ASSISTANCE COMMITTEE (2003). Biodiversity and equality between women and men. In *Tipsheets for Improving Gender Equality*. Available from http://www1.oecd.org/dac/gender/htm/tipsheets.htm. Paris.

▸ RAMSAR CONVENTION BUREAU and UNITED NATIONS EDUCATIONAL, SCIENTIFIC AND CULTURAL ORGANIZATION (2003). *The Ramsar Convention on Wetlands*. Internet site http://www.ramsar.org. Geneva.

▸ UNITED NATIONS (2001). *Indicators of Sustainable Development: Guidelines and Methodologies*. Sales No. E.01.II.A.6. Available from http://www.un.org/esa/sustdev/natlinfo/indicators/isd.htm.

▸ UNITED NATIONS. ECONOMIC COMMISSION FOR EUROPE. CONFERENCE OF EUROPEAN STATISTICS (1989). *ECE Standard Statistical Classification of Land Use*. Geneva. Available from http://www.unescap.org/stat/envstat/stwes-class-landuse.pdf.

▸ UNITED NATIONS EDUCATIONAL, SCIENTIFIC AND CULTURAL ORGANIZATION (2003). *The MAB Programme: World Network of Biosphere Reserves*. Internet site http://www.unesco.org/mab/wnbr.htm. Paris.

▸ UNITED NATIONS EDUCATIONAL, SCIENTIFIC AND CULTURAL ORGANIZATION (2003). *World Heritage*. Internet site http://whc.unesco.org/nwhc/pages/home/pages/homepage.htm. Paris.

▸ UNITED NATIONS ENVIRONMENT PROGRAMME– WORLD CONSERVATION MONITORING CENTRE (2003). *World Database on Protected Areas*. Internet site http://sea.unep-wcmc.org . Cambridge, United Kingdom.

▸ WORLD CONSERVATION UNION (IUCN). *Biodiversity Policy Coordination Division*. Internet site http://www.iucn.org/themes/biodiversity.

▸ WORLD CONSERVATION UNION, WORLD COMMISSION OF PROTECTED AREAS with the assistance of the WORLD CONSERVATION MONITORING CENTRE (1994). *Guidelines for Protected Area Management Categories*. Cambridge, United Kingdom. Available from http://www.wcmc.org.uk/protected_area/categories/eng.

AGENCIES

Ministries of environment
United Nations Environment Programme, World Conservation Monitoring Centre
IUCN–World Conservation Union

27 ENERGY USE (KILOGRAM OIL EQUIVALENT) PER $1 GROSS DOMESTIC PRODUCT (PPP)

DEFINITION

Energy use (kilogram oil equivalent) per $1 gross domestic product (PPP) is commercial energy use measured in units of oil equivalent per $1 of gross domestic product converted from national currencies using purchasing power parity conversion factors.

GOAL AND TARGET ADDRESSED

Goal 7. Ensure environmental sustainability
Target 9. Integrate the principles of sustainable development into country policies and programmes and reverse the loss of environmental resources

RATIONALE

The indicator provides a measure of energy intensity (it is the inverse of energy efficiency). Differences in this ratio over time and across countries reflect structural changes in the economy, changes in the energy efficiency of particular sectors and differences in fuel mixes. In principle, the lower the ratio, the better the energy efficiency.

METHOD OF COMPUTATION

Total commercial energy consumption is converted to metric ton oil equivalence using standard tables. GDP data must be converted using PPP tables so that real output is compared with real energy input. National total GDP is deflated (currently to 1995 US PPP dollars) by reference to PPP tables derived from the International Comparison Programme. Energy input is divided by GDP to derive the ratio.

DATA COLLECTION AND SOURCE

Energy consumption is calculated from national energy balance sheets. Real GDP comes from the national income accounts deflated by reference to PPP tables prepared by the International Comparison Programme. Traditional fuels, such as animal and vegetable waste, fuel wood and charcoal, are excluded.

PERIODICITY OF MEASUREMENT

Data are available annually.

DISAGGREGATION ISSUES

This is a relatively crude indicator and needs to be broken down by sector of industry to be interpreted.

COMMENTS AND LIMITATIONS

As the input is commercial energy, it should be compared with the output from that energy, deflated by the purchasing power parities relevant to that output. Changes in the ratio over time are influenced almost as much by changes in the structure of the economy as by changes in sectoral energy intensities.

REFERENCES AND INTERNATIONAL DATA COMPARISONS

▸ INTERNATIONAL ENERGY AGENCY (2003). Internet site http://www.iea.org . Paris.

▸ INTERNATIONAL ENERGY AGENCY (annual). *Energy Balances of Non-OECD Countries*. Paris.

▸ INTERNATIONAL ENERGY AGENCY (annual). *Energy Balances of OECD Countries*. Paris.

▸ UNITED NATIONS (1987). *Energy Statistics – Definitions, Units of Measure and Conversion Factors*, Series F, No. 44. Sales No. E.86.XVII.21. Available from http://unstats.un.org/unsd/ pubs. (E, F, R, S)

▸ UNITED NATIONS (2001). *Indicators of Sustainable Development: Guidelines and Methodologies*. Department of Economic and Social Affairs, Division for Sustainable Development Sales No. E.01.II.A.6. Available from http://www.un.org/esa/sustdev/natlinfo/indicators/isd.htm.

▸ UNITED NATIONS (2003). Energy Statistics. Internet site http://unstats.un.org/unsd/energy.

▸ UNITED NATIONS (2003). *Millennium Indicators Database*. Statistics Division Internet site http://millenniumindicators.un.org.

▸ UNITED NATIONS. COMMISSION OF THE EUROPEAN COMMUNITIES, INTERNATIONAL MONETARY FUND, ORGANISATION FOR ECONOMIC CO-OPERATION AND DEVELOPMENT and WORLD BANK (1994). *System of National Accounts 1993 (SNA 1993)*, Series F, No.2, Rev. 4. Sales No. E.94.XVII.4. Available with updates from http://unstats. un.org/unsd/sna1993.

▸ WORLD BANK (2003 and annual). *World Development Indicators*. Print and CD-ROM. Washington, D.C. Available in part from http://www.worldbank.org/data .

AGENCIES

International Energy Agency
World Bank
United Nations Statistics Division

28 CARBON DIOXIDE EMISSIONS PER CAPITA AND CONSUMPTION OF OZONE-DEPLETING CHLOROFLUORO-CARBONS (ODP TONS)

DEFINITION

Carbon dioxide emissions per capita is the total amount of carbon dioxide emitted by a country as a consequence of human (production and consumption) activities, divided by the population of the country. In the global carbon dioxide emission estimates of the Carbon Dioxide Information Analysis Center of Oak Ridge National Laboratory in the United States, the calculated country emissions of carbon dioxide include emissions from consumption of solid, liquid and gas fuels; cement production; and gas flaring. National reporting to the United Nations Framework Convention on Climate Change, which follows the Intergovernmental Panel on Climate Change guidelines, is based on national emission inventories and covers all sources of anthropogenic carbon dioxide emissions as well as carbon sinks (such as forests).

Consumption of ozone-depleting chlorofluorocarbons (CFCs) in ODP (ozone-depleting potential) tons is the sum of the consumption of the weighted tons of the individual substances in the group—metric tons of the individual substance (defined in the Montreal Protocol on Substances that Deplete the Ozone Layer) multiplied by its ozone-depleting potential. An *ozone-depleting substance* is any substance containing chlorine or bromine that destroys the stratospheric ozone layer. The stratospheric ozone layer absorbs most of the biologically damaging ultraviolet radiation.

GOAL AND TARGET ADDRESSED

Goal 7. Ensure environmental sustainability
Target 9. Integrate the principles of sustainable development into country policies and programmes and reverse the loss of environmental resources

RATIONALE

The indicators signify the commitment to reducing carbon dioxide emissions and progress in phasing out the consumption of CFCs by countries that have ratified the Montreal Protocol. Carbon dioxide emissions are largely a by-product of energy production and use. They account for the largest share of greenhouse gases associated with global warming.

The Vienna Convention for the Protection of the Ozone Layer (1985) and the Montreal Protocol (1987) are now recognized as having been successful in preventing the global environmental catastrophe that could have been caused by stratospheric ozone depletion. The Montreal Protocol aims to reduce and eventually eliminate the emissions of anthropogenic ozone-depleting substances by ceasing their production and consumption. The phasing out of ozone-depleting substances and their replacement with less harmful substances or new processes are aimed at the recovery of the ozone layer.

CFCs are considered most representative of the protocol's efforts to phase out the use of ozone-depleting substances since they were the first to be targeted for elimination.

METHOD OF COMPUTATION

Carbon dioxide emissions per capita are calculated by dividing carbon dioxide emissions by the number of people in the national population. Carbon dioxide emission estimates from 1950 to the present are derived primarily from energy statistics published by the United Nations, using the methods outlined in "Carbon dioxide emissions from fossil fuels: a procedure for estimation and results for 1950–82". National reporting to the United Nations Framework Convention on Climate Change is based on the Intergovernmental Panel on Climate Change guidelines. Carbon dioxide emissions can be expressed in terms of carbon dioxide or converted to carbon content.

The consumption of CFCs is the national production plus imports, minus exports, minus destroyed quantities, minus feedstock uses of individual CFCs. National annual consumption of CFCs is the sum of the weighted tons (consumption in metric tons multiplied by the estimated ozone-depleting potential) of the individual CFCs.

DATA COLLECTION AND SOURCE
National carbon dioxide emissions are estimated from detailed data on emission sources, using source-specific emission factors. Emission inventories are usually compiled by energy or environment ministries. Annex I parties (developed countries) to the United Nations Framework Convention on Climate Change submit their data on greenhouse gas emissions to the organization's secretariat through an annual reporting format. Reporting of Non-annex I parties is voluntary and occasional. Where national emission inventories are absent, official sources are supplemented by other sources and estimates.

Estimation of the consumption of CFCs requires data on national production plus imports, minus exports, minus stocks destroyed. Those can be derived from national production and international trade statistics.

PERIODICITY OF MEASUREMENT
Data are usually collected annually.

COMMENTS AND LIMITATIONS
For carbon dioxide emissions, trend data are more reliable than data comparisons between countries.

For ozone depletion, the indicator does not reveal much about current trends in deterioration of the ozone layer owing to delays in ecosystem response.

REFERENCES AND INTERNATIONAL DATA COMPARISONS
▸ CARBON DIOXIDE INFORMATION ANALYSIS CENTRE (CDIAC) (2003). *Global, Regional, and National Fossil Fuel CO2 Emissions*: http://cdiac.ornl.gov/trends/emis/meth_reg.htm. Oak Ridge, Tennessee.
▸ CARBON DIOXIDE INFORMATION ANALYSIS CENTRE (CDIAC) (2003). Internet site http://cdiac.esd.ornl.gov/. Oak Ridge, Tennessee.
▸ MARLAND, G., and R.M. ROTTY (1984). Carbon dioxide emissions from fossil fuels: a procedure for estimation and results for 1950–82. *Tellus*, 36(B): 232–61.
▸ UNITED NATIONS (1996). *Glossary of Environmental Statistics*, Series F, No. 67 (United Nations publication, Sales No. E.96.XVII.12). Available from http://unstats.un.org/unsd/pubs. (A, C, E, F, R, S)
▸ UNITED NATIONS (2001). *Indicators of Sustainable Development: Guidelines and Methodologies*. Sales No. E.01.II.A.6. Available from http://www.un.org/esa/sustdev/natlinfo/indicators/isd.htm.
▸ UNITED NATIONS ENVIRONMENT PROGRAMME (2002). *Production and Consumption of Ozone-Depleting Substances under the Montreal Protocol, 1986-2000*. Available from http://www.unep.ch/ozone/15-year-data-report.pdf. Nairobi.
▸ UNITED NATIONS ENVIRONMENT PROGRAMME (2003). *The Ozone Secretariat*. Internet site http://www.unep.org/ozone/. Nairobi.
▸ UNITED NATIONS FRAMEWORK CONVENTION ON CLIMATE CHANGE (2003). *Greenhouse Gas Inventory Database (GHG)*. Internet site http://ghg.unfccc.int. Bonn, Germany.
▸ UNITED NATIONS FRAMEWORK CONVENTION ON CLIMATE CHANGE (2003). Internet site http://www.unfccc.int. Bonn, Germany.
▸ WORLD BANK (2003 and annual). *World Development Indicators*. Print and CD-ROM. Washington, D.C. Available in part from http://www.worldbank.org/data.
▸ WORLD METEOROLOGICAL ORGANIZATION AND UNITED NATIONS ENVIRONMENT PROGRAMME. INTER-GOVERNMENTAL PANEL ON CLIMATE CHANGE (2003). Internet site http://www.ipcc.ch.

Geneva.

▸ **WORLD RESOURCE INSTITUTE** (2003). *EarthTrends: The Environment Information Portal*. Internet site http://earthtrends.wri.org. Washington, D.C.

AGENCIES

Carbon dioxide:
United Nations Framework Convention on Climate Change
United Nations Statistics Division

Chlorofluorocarbons:
United Nations Environment Programme, Ozone Secretariat

29 PROPORTION OF THE POPULATION USING SOLID FUELS

DEFINITION
Proportion of population using solid fuels is the proportion of the population that relies on biomass (wood, charcoal, crop residues and dung) and coal as the primary source of domestic energy for cooking and heating.

GOAL AND TARGET ADDRESSED
Goal 7. Ensure environmental sustainability
Target 9. Integrate the principles of sustainable development into country policies and programmes and reverse the loss of environmental resources

RATIONALE
Incomplete and inefficient combustion of solid fuels results in the emission of hundreds of compounds, many of which are health-damaging pollutants or greenhouse gases that contribute to global climate change. There are also important linkages between household solid fuel use, indoor air pollution, deforestation and soil erosion and greenhouse gas emissions. Exposure to indoor air pollution is a complex phenomenon and depends on interactions of pollution source (fuel and stove type), pollution dispersion (housing and ventilation) and the time-activity budget of household

members. The type of fuel and participation in cooking tasks have consistently been the most important predictors of exposure.

METHOD OF COMPUTATION
The indicator is computed as the ratio of households using one or more unprocessed solid fuels (dung and crop residues, wood, charcoal, and coal) for cooking and heating, to the total population, expressed as a percentage.

DATA COLLECTION AND SOURCE
Data can be derived from household surveys, such as Living Standard Measurement study surveys and Demographic and Health Surveys and from population censuses. Standard questions for inclusion in all nationally representative household surveys have not yet been developed and no internationally comparable data are available.

GENDER ISSUES
More than half the world's households cook with unprocessed solid fuels, exposing primarily women and children to indoor air pollution, which can result in serious health problems, such as acute respiratory diseases. In addition, women spend more time than men gathering wood for fuel.

COMMENTS AND LIMITATIONS
Development of standard questions for inclusion in all nationally representative household surveys and censuses is needed to obtain data for calculating the indicator and allowing comparisons across countries.

Since the use of solid fuels affects both the environment and the population as a whole and the health status of those directly exposed, guidelines should clearly set definitions and measurement standards for what is intended by "exposure".

REFERENCES AND INTERNATIONAL DATA COMPARISONS
▸ **BRUCE, NIGEL, ROGELIO PEREZ-PADILLA** and

Rachel Albalak (2000). Indoor air pollution in developing countries: a major environmental and public health challenge. *Bulletin of the World Health Organization* 78 (9), 1078-1092 Geneva.

▸ Stakeholder Forum (2002). Earth Summit Forum 2002. Internet site http://www.earth summit2002.org/es/issues/gender/gender.htm.

▸ United Nations (1982). *Concepts and Methods in Energy Statistics, with Special Reference to Energy Accounts and Balances: A Technical Report*, Series F, No. 29. Sales No. E.82.XVII.13 and corrigendum. Available from http://unstats.un.org/unsd/pubs (E, F, R).

▸ United Nations (1987). *Energy Statistics – Definitions, Units of Measure and Conversion Factors*, Series F, No. 44. Sales No. E.86.XVII.21. Available from http://unstats.un.org/unsd/pubs (E, F, R, S).

▸ World Bank (2003). *Briefing Notes on Gender and Development - Energy*. Available from http://www.worldbank.org/gender/resources/briefing. Washington, D.C.

▸ World Health Organization (2002). *World Health Report 2002 – Reducing Risks, Promoting Healthy Life*. Geneva. Available from http://www.who.int/whr/en.

The World Health Organization has produced estimates of regional aggregates for this indicator. However, no country data series are available to allow comparison across countries or assessment of trends.

AGENCIES
National statistical offices
World Health Organization

30 PROPORTION OF POPULATION WITH SUSTAINABLE ACCESS TO AN IMPROVED WATER SOURCE, URBAN AND RURAL

DEFINITION
The *proportion of the population with sustainable access to an improved water source, urban and rural*, is the percentage of the population who use any of the following types of water supply for drinking: piped water, public tap, borehole or pump, protected well, protected spring or rainwater. Improved water sources do not include vendor-provided water, bottled water, tanker trucks or unprotected wells and springs.

GOAL AND TARGET ADDRESSED
Goal 7: Ensure environmental sustainability.
Target 10: Halve, by 2015, the proportion of people without sustainable access to safe drinking water and basic sanitation.

RATIONALE
The indicator monitors access to improved water sources based on the assumption that improved sources are more likely to provide safe water. Unsafe water is the direct cause of many diseases in developing countries.

METHOD OF COMPUTATION
The indicator is computed as the ratio of the number of people who use piped water, public tap, borehole or pump, protected well, protected spring or rainwater to the total population, expressed as a percentage. The same method applies for the urban and rural breakdown.

Access to safe water refers to the percentage of the population with reasonable access to an adequate supply of safe water in their dwelling or within a convenient distance of their dwelling. The *Global Water Supply and Sanitation Assessment 2000 Report* defines *reasonable access* as "the availability of 20 litres per capita per day at a distance no longer than 1,000 metres". However, access and volume of drinking water are difficult to measure, so sources of drinking water that are thought to provide safe water are used as a proxy.

The United Nations Children's Fund (UNICEF) and the World Health Organization (WHO), through the Joint Monitoring Programme, assess trends in "access to improved drinking water sources" by drawing a regression line through the available household survey and census data for each country (details are available at http://www.childinfo.org). Regional and global estimates are aggregated from the national estimates, using population-weighted averages.

DATA COLLECTION AND SOURCE

Since the late 1990s, data have routinely been collected at the national and subnational levels in more than 100 countries using censuses and surveys by national Governments, often with support from international development agencies. Two data sources are common: administrative or infrastructure data that report on new and existing facilities, and data from household surveys, including Multiple Indicator Cluster Surveys, Demographic and Health Surveys and Living Standards Measurement study surveys. Before the population-based data were available, provider-based data were used.

Evidence suggests that data from surveys are more reliable than administrative records and provide information on facilities actually used by the population.

PERIODICITY OF MEASUREMENT

Administrative data are often available annually. Household surveys are generally conducted every three to five years.

WHO and UNICEF annually compile international data and prepare regional and global estimates based on household survey data.

GENDER ISSUES

Women and men usually have different roles in water and sanitation activities. The differences are particularly pronounced in rural areas. Women are most often the users, providers and managers of water in rural households and the guardians of household hygiene. If a water system breaks down, women are more likely to be affected than men because they have to travel farther for water or use other means to meet the household's water and sanitation needs.

DISAGGREGATION ISSUES

The indicator should be monitored separately for urban and rural areas. Because of national differences in characteristics that distinguish urban from rural areas, the distinction between urban and rural population is not amenable to a single definition applicable to all countries. National definitions are most commonly based on size of locality, with rural population as the residual of population that is not considered urban.

COMMENTS AND LIMITATIONS

When data from administrative sources are used, they generally refer to existing sources, whether used or not. Despite official WHO definitions, the judgment about whether a water source is safe is often subjective. In addition, the existence of a water supply does not necessarily mean that it is safe or that local people use it. For those and other reasons, household survey data are generally better than administrative data, since survey data are based on actual use of sources by the surveyed population rather than the simple existence of the sources.

While access is the most reasonable indicator for water supply, it still involves severe methodological and practical problems. Among them:

- The data are not routinely collected by "the sector" but by others outside the sector as part of more general surveys.
- Water quality is not systematically addressed.
- The timing of collection and analysis of

household survey data is irregular, with long intervals between surveys

REFERENCES AND INTERNATIONAL DATA COMPARISONS

▸ **ORC MACRO** (2003). *Demographic and Health Surveys – Providing Information for Informed Decisions in Population, Health and Nutrition*. Internet site http://www.measuredhs.com. Calverton, Maryland.

▸ **UNITED NATIONS** (1998). *Principles and Recommendations for Population and Housing Censuses, Revision 1*, Series M, No. 67, Rev. 1. Sales No. E.98.XVII.1. Available from http://unstats.un.org/unsd/pubs (A, E, F, S).

▸ **UNITED NATIONS** (2001). *Indicators of Sustainable Development: Guidelines and Methodologies*. Sales No. E.01.II.A.6. Available from http://www.un.org/esa/sustdev/natlinfo/indicators/isd.htm.

▸ **UNITED NATIONS** (2003). *Millennium Indicators Database*. Statistics Division Internet site http://millenniumindicators.un.org.

▸ **UNITED NATIONS CHILDREN'S FUND** (2003). *Progress since the World Summit for Children*. New York. Available from http://www.childinfo.org.

▸ **UNITED NATIONS CHILDREN'S FUND** (annual). *The State of the World's Children*. New York.

▸ **WORLD BANK** (2003 and annual). *World Development Indicators*. Print and CD-ROM. Washington, D.C. Available in part from http://www.worldbank.org/data.

▸ **WORLD BANK** (2003). *Briefing Notes on Gender Development - Water and Sanitation*. Washington, D.C. Available from http://www.worldbank.org/gender/resources/briefing.

▸ **WORLD BANK** (2003). *The Living Standards Measurement Study of the World Bank* (LSMS). Internet site http://www.worldbank.org/lsms. Washington, D.C.

▸ **WORLD BANK** (2003). *Toolkit on Gender in Water and Sanitation*. Washington, D.C. Available from http://www.worldbank.org/gender/resources/sectoraltools.htm.

▸ **WORLD HEALTH ORGANIZATION** (2002 and annual). *World Health Report*. Geneva. Available from http://www.who.int/whr/en.

▸ **WORLD HEALTH ORGANIZATION AND UNITED NATIONS CHILDREN'S FUND** (2000). *Global Water Supply and Sanitation Assessment 2000 Report*, pp.77-78. Geneva. Available from http://www.who.int/docstore/water_sanitation_health/Globassessment/GlobalTOC.htm.

AGENCIES
National statistical offices
United Nations Children's Fund
World Health Organization

31 PROPORTION OF POPULATION WITH ACCESS TO IMPROVED SANITATION, URBAN AND RURAL

DEFINITION
Proportion of the urban and rural population with access to improved sanitation refers to the percentage of the population with access to facilities that hygienically separate human excreta from human, animal and insect contact. Facilities such as sewers or septic tanks, poor-flush latrines and simple pit or ventilated improved pit latrines are assumed to be adequate, provided that they are not public, according to the World Health Organization and United Nations Children's Fund's *Global Water Supply and Sanitation Assessment 2000 Report*. To be effective, facilities must be correctly constructed and properly maintained.

GOAL AND TARGET ADDRESSED
Goal 7. Ensure environmental sustainability
Target 10. Halve, by 2015, the proportion of people without sustainable access to safe drinking water and basic sanitation

RATIONALE
Good sanitation is important for urban and rural populations, but the risks are greater in urban

areas where it is more difficult to avoid contact with waste.

METHOD OF COMPUTATION
The indicator is computed as the ratio of the number of people in urban or rural areas with access to improved excreta-disposal facilities to the total urban or rural population, expressed as a percentage.

DATA COLLECTION AND SOURCE
Since the late 1990s, data have routinely been collected at national and subnational levels in more than 100 countries using censuses and surveys by national Governments, often with support from international development agencies. Two data sources are common: administrative or infrastructure data that report on new and existing facilities, and data from household surveys including Multiple Indicator Cluster Surveys, Demographic and Health Surveys, and LSMS surveys. Before those population-based data were available, provider-based data were used.

Evidence suggests that data from surveys are more reliable than administrative records and provide information on facilities actually used by the population.

Rural and urban population statistics come directly from population censuses.

PERIODICITY OF MEASUREMENT
Administrative data are often available annually. Household surveys are generally conducted every three to five years. WHO and UNICEF annually compile international data and prepare regional and global estimates based on household survey data.

GENDER ISSUES
Women and men usually have different roles in water and sanitation activities. The differences are particularly pronounced in rural areas. Women are most often the users, providers and managers of water in rural house-holds and the guardians of household hygiene. If a water system breaks down, women are more likely to be affected than men because they have to travel farther for water or use other means to meet the household's water and sanitation needs.

DISAGGREGATION ISSUES
The indicator should be monitored separately for urban and rural areas. Owing to national differences in characteristics that distinguish urban from rural areas, the distinction between urban and rural population is not amenable to a single definition applicable to all countries. National definitions are most commonly based on size of locality, with rural population as the residual of population that is not considered urban.

COMMENTS AND LIMITATIONS
When data are from administrative sources, they generally refer to existing sanitation facilities, whether used or not. Household survey data are therefore generally better than administrative data, since survey data are based on actual use of facilities by the surveyed population rather than the simple existence of the facilities.

While access is the most reasonable indicator for sanitation facilities, it still involves severe methodological and practical problems, including the following:
- The data are not routinely collected by "the sector" but by others outside the sector as part of more general surveys
- Facility quality is not systematically addressed
- The timing of collection and analysis of household survey data is irregular, with long intervals between surveys

The definition of *access to improved sanitation facilities* and methods for assessing it are even more contentious than those for water, with national definitions of "acceptable" sanitation varying widely.

REFERENCES AND INTERNATIONAL DATA COMPARISONS

▸ **ORC Macro** (2003). *Demographic and Health Surveys – Providing Information for Informed Decisions in Population, Health and Nutrition*. Internet site http://www.measuredhs.com. Calverton, Maryland.

▸ **United Nations** (1998). *Principles and Recommendations for Population and Housing Censuses, Revision 1*, Series M, No. 67, Rev. 1. Sales No. E.98.XVII.1. Available from http://unstats.un.org/unsd/pubs (A, E, F, S).

▸ **United Nations** (2001). *Indicators of Sustainable Development: Guidelines and Methodologies*. Sales No. E.01.II.A.6. Available from http://www.un.org/esa/sustdev/natlinfo/indicators/isd.htm.

▸ **United Nations** (2003). *Millennium Indicators Database*. Statistics Division Internet site http://millenniumindicators.un.org.

▸ **United Nations Children's Fund** (2003). *Progress since the World Summit for Children*. New York. Available from http://www.childinfo.org .

▸ **World Bank** (2003) *The Living Standards Measurement Study of the World Bank* (LSMS). Internet site http://www.worldbank.org/lsms. Washington, D.C.

▸ **World Health Organization and United Nations Children's Fund** (2000). *Global Water Supply and Sanitation Assessment 2000 Report*. Geneva. Available from http://www.who.int/docstore/ water_sanitation_health/Globassessment/GlobalTOC.htm .

AGENCIES

National statistical offices
United Nations Children's Fund
World Health Organization

32 PROPORTION OF HOUSEHOLDS WITH ACCESS TO SECURE TENURE

DEFINITION

The *proportion of households with access to secure tenure* is 1 minus the percentage of the urban population that lives in slums. In the absence of data on number of slum dwellers, the United Nations Human Settlements Programme (UN-HABITAT) produces estimates based on a definition of slums as agreed by the Expert Group Meeting on Urban Indicators in 2002. Those indicators will be adjusted, and the definitions of secure tenure and slums will be refined through future consultations with Expert Group Meeting participants and their related networks of professionals.

Secure tenure refers to households that own or are purchasing their homes, are renting privately or are in social housing or subtenancy. Households without secure tenure are defined as *squatters* (whether or not they pay rent), *homeless* and *households with no formal agreement*.

UN-HABITAT defines a *slum* household as a group of individuals living under the same roof who lack one or more (in some cities, two or more) of the following conditions: security of tenure, structural quality and durability of dwellings, access to safe water, access to sanitation facilities and sufficient living area.

GOAL AND TARGET ADDRESSED

Goal 7. Ensure environmental sustainability
Target 11. By 2020, to have achieved a significant improvement in the lives of at least 100 million slum dwellers

RATIONALE

The indicator is intended to provide an overview of the share of urban population living in conditions of poverty and physical and environmental deprivation.

METHOD OF COMPUTATION

The indicator is computed as 1 minus the ratio of the number of households in urban areas that lack one or more of the above-mentioned conditions listed under "Definition" to the number of urban households, expressed as a percentage.

DATA COLLECTION AND SOURCE

Data come mainly from household surveys such as the Demographic and Health Surveys, Multiple Indicator Cluster Surveys and Joint Monitoring Programme questionnaires. In countries without such data from surveys, data can be derived from population and housing censuses, which usually include questions about housing tenure.

UN-HABITAT produces slum population estimates based on those national sources for assessing regional and global trends.

PERIODICITY OF MEASUREMENT

Household surveys are generally conducted every three to five years. Censuses are conducted every 10 years.

GENDER ISSUES

For women (more than for men), housing—beyond basic shelter—also often functions as an important place of employment and social interaction, and a place to care for children. It may offer respite from social instability and violence. Discriminatory social and economic practices within and outside the household may result in women being excluded from many aspects of housing, including policy development, control over housing resources, rights of inheritance and ownership, community organizing or the construction of housing. Such exclusion can threaten women's security of tenure by preventing women from owning, inheriting, leasing, renting or remaining in housing and on land.

COMMENTS AND LIMITATIONS

Data are not yet generally available.

REFERENCES AND INTERNATIONAL DATA COMPARISONS

▸ CENTER ON HOUSING RIGHTS AND EVICTIONS (2003). Women and housing rights. In *Housing Rights*. Geneva. Available from http://www.cohre.org/hrframe.htm.
▸ UNITED NATIONS (2003). *Millennium Indicators Database*. Statistics Division Internet site http://millenniumindicators.un.org.
▸ UNITED NATIONS. COMMISSION ON HUMAN RIGHTS. Women's equal ownership of, access to and control over land and the equal rights to own property and to adequate housing. *Official Records of the Economic and Social Council, Fifty-sixth Session Supplemjent No. 3* (E/200/23-E/CN.4/2000/167), resolution 2000/13. Geneva. Available from http://www.unhabitat.org/programmes/landtenure/13.asp.
▸ UNITED NATIONS HUMAN SETTLEMENTS PROGRAMME (UN-HABITAT) (2002). Expert Group Meeting on Urban Indicators – Secure Tenure, Slums and Global Sample of Cities. Nairobi. Available from http://www.unhabitat.org/programmes/guo/documents/EGM final report 4 Dec 02.pdf.
▸ UNITED NATIONS HUMAN SETTLEMENTS PROGRAMME (UN-HABITAT) (2003). *Global Urban Observatory*. Internet site http://www.unhabitat.org/programmes/guo. Nairobi.
▸ UNITED NATIONS HUMAN SETTLEMENTS PROGRAMME (UN-HABITAT) (2003). *Guide to Monitoring Target 11: Improving the Lives of 100 Million Slum Dwellers–Progress towards the Millennium Development Goals*. Nairobi. Available from http://www.unhabitat.org/mdg.
▸ UNITED NATIONS HUMAN SETTLEMENTS PROGRAMME (UN-HABITAT) (2003). The Global Campaign for Secure Tenure. Internet site http://www.unhabitat.org/campaigns/tenure. Nairobi.

UN-HABITAT produces regional and global estimates of percentage of slum dwellers based on national data. Internationally comparable data series at country level have not yet been produced.

AGENCY

United Nations Human Settlements Programme

33 NET ODA, TOTAL AND TO THE LEAST DEVELOPED COUNTRIES, AS A PERCENTAGE OF OECD/DAC DONORS' GROSS NATIONAL INCOME

DEFINITION

Official development assistance comprises grants or loans to developing countries and territories on the Organisation for Economic Co-operation and Development/Development Assistance Committee (OECD/DAC) list of aid recipients that are undertaken by the official sector with promotion of economic development and welfare as the main objective and at concessional financial terms (if a loan, having a grant element of at least 25 per cent). Technical cooperation is included. Grants, loans and credits for military purposes are excluded. Also excluded is aid to more advanced developing and transition countries as determined by DAC.

Donors' gross national income (GNI) at market prices is the sum of gross primary incomes receivable by resident institutional units and sectors. GNI at market prices was called gross national product (GNP) in the 1953 System of National Accounts. In contrast to gross domestic product (GDP), GNI is a concept of income (primary income) rather than value added.

The General Assembly, on the recommendation of the Committee for Development Policy, through the Economic and Social Council, decides on the countries to be included in the list of *least developed countries* (LDCs). As of January 2004, the list included the following countries, by region: *Africa*: Angola, Benin, Burkina Faso, Burundi, Cape Verde, Central African Republic, Chad, Comoros, Democratic Republic of the Congo, Djibouti, Equatorial Guinea, Eritrea, Ethiopia, Gambia, Guinea, Guinea-Bissau, Lesotho, Liberia, Madagascar, Malawi, Mali, Mauritania, Mozambique, the Niger, Rwanda, Saõ Tomé and Principe, Senegal, Sierra Leone, Somalia, the Sudan, Togo, Uganda, the United Republic of Tanzania and Zambia; *Asia and the Pacific*: Afghanistan, Bangladesh, Bhutan, Cambodia, Kiribati, the Lao People's Democratic Republic, Maldives, Myanmar, Nepal, Samoa, Solomon Islands, Timor Leste, Tuvalu, Vanuatu and Yemen; *Latin America and the Caribbean*: Haiti.

GOAL AND TARGETS ADDRESSED

Goal 8. Develop a global partnership for development

Target 12. Develop further an open, rule-based, predictable, non-discriminatory trading and financial system. Includes a commitment to good governance, development and poverty reduction—both nationally and internationally

Target 13. Address the special needs of the least developed countries. Includes: tariff and quota-free access for least developed countries' exports; enhanced programme of debt relief for heavily indebted poor countries and cancellation of official bilateral debt; and more generous ODA for countries committed to poverty reduction

Target 14. Address the special needs of landlocked countries and small island developing States (through the Programme of Action for the Sustainable Development of Small Island Developing States and the outcome of the twenty-second special session of the General Assembly)

Target 15. Deal comprehensively with the debt problems of developing countries through national and international measures in order to make debt sustainable in the long term

RATIONALE

Goal 8 addresses the way developed countries can assist developing countries to achieve the other seven goals through more development assistance, improved access to markets and debt relief. The International Conference on Financing for Development, held in Monterrey, Mexico in 2002, stimulated commitments from major donors to start to reverse the decline in official development assistance and focus more on poverty reduction, education and health to help countries realize the Millennium Development Goals.

METHOD OF COMPUTATION

GNI is equal to GDP (which at market prices represents the final result of the production activity of resident producer units) less primary incomes payable to non-resident units plus primary incomes receivable from non-resident units. In other words, GNI is equal to GDP less taxes (less subsidies) on production and imports, compensation of employees and property income payable to the rest of the world plus the corresponding items receivable from the rest of the world.

DATA COLLECTION AND SOURCE

Data are compiled by the Development Assistance Committee of OECD.

PERIODICITY OF MEASUREMENT

Annual.

REFERENCES AND INTERNATIONAL DATA COMPARISONS

▸ ORGANISATION FOR ECONOMIC CO-OPERATION AND DEVELOPMENT. DEVELOPMENT ASSISTANCE COMMITTEE (2003). Internet site http://www.oecd.org/dac . Paris.

▸ ORGANISATION FOR ECONOMIC CO-OPERATION AND DEVELOPMENT. DEVELOPMENT ASSISTANCE COMMITTEE (annual). *Development Co-operation Report*. Paris.

▸ ORGANISATION FOR ECONOMIC CO-OPERATION AND DEVELOPMENT. DEVELOPMENT ASSISTANCE COMMITTEE (annual). *International Development Statistics*. CD-ROM. Paris.

▸ UNITED NATIONS (2003). *Millennium Indicators Database*. Statistics Division Internet site http://millenniumindicators.un.org.

▸ UNITED NATIONS, COMMISSION OF THE EUROPEAN COMMUNITIES, INTERNATIONAL MONETARY FUND, ORGANISATION FOR ECONOMIC CO-OPERATION and DEVELOPMENT AND WORLD BANK (1994). *System of National Accounts 1993 (SNA 1993)*, Series F, No.2, Rev. 4. Sales No. E.94.XVII.4. Available with updates at http://unstats. un.org/unsd/sna1993.

▸ UNITED NATIONS OFFICE OF THE HIGH REPRESENTATIVE FOR THE LEAST DEVELOPED COUNTRIES, LANDLOCKED DEVELOPING COUNTRIES AND SMALL ISLAND DEVELOPING STATES (2003). Internet site http://www.un.org/ohrlls.

AGENCY

Organisation for Economic Co-operation and Development, Development Assistance Committee

34 PROPORTION OF TOTAL BILATERAL, SECTOR-ALLOCABLE ODA OF OECD/ DAC DONORS TO BASIC SOCIAL SERVICES (BASIC EDUCATION, PRIMARY HEALTH CARE, NUTRITION, SAFE WATER AND SANITATION)

DEFINITION

Official development assistance comprises grants or loans to developing countries and territories on the OECD Development Assistance Committee list of aid recipients that are undertaken by the official sector with promotion of economic development and welfare as the main objective and at concessional financial terms (if a loan, having a grant element of at least 25 per cent). Technical cooperation is included. Grants, loans and credits for military purposes are excluded. Also excluded is aid to more advanced developing and transition countries as determined by DAC. *Bilateral official development assistance* is from one country to another.

Basic education comprises primary education, basic life skills for youth and adults and early childhood education. *Primary health care* includes basic health care, basic health infrastructure, basic nutrition, infectious disease control, health education and health personnel development. (For safe water and sanitation, see INDICATORS 30 and 31.)

GOAL AND TARGETS ADDRESSED

Goal 8. Develop a global partnership for development

Target 12. Develop further an open, rule-based, predictable, non-discriminatory trading and financial system. Includes a commitment to good governance, development and poverty reduction—both nationally and internationally.

Target 13. Address the special needs of the least developed countries. Includes: tariff and quota-free access for least developed countries' exports; enhanced programme of debt relief for heavily indebted poor countries and cancellation of official bilateral debt; and more generous ODA for countries committed to poverty reduction

Target 14. Address the special needs of landlocked countries and small island developing States (through the Programme of Action for the Sustainable Development of Small Island Developing States and the outcome of the twenty-second special session of the General Assembly)

Target 15. Deal comprehensively with the debt problems of developing countries through national and international measures in order to make debt sustainable in the long term

RATIONALE

The World Summit on Social Development at Copenhagen in 1995 suggested the possibility of "mutual commitment between interested developed and developing country partners to allocate, on average, 20 per cent of ODA and 20 per cent of the national budget, respectively, to basic social programmes". These programmes comprise basic education, basic health, population and reproductive health programmes, and poverty-focused water and sanitation projects.

DATA COLLECTION AND SOURCE

Compiled by the Development Assistance Committee of the OECD.

PERIODICITY OF MEASUREMENT

Annual.

COMMENTS AND LIMITATIONS

Aid to water supply and sanitation is defined as part of basic social services only if poverty focused.

REFERENCES AND INTERNATIONAL DATA COMPARISONS

▶ ORGANISATION FOR ECONOMIC CO-OPERATION AND DEVELOPMENT. DEVELOPMENT ASSISTANCE COMMITTEE (2003). Internet site http://www.oecd.org/dac. Under Topics, select: Aid statistics, Aid effectiveness and donor practices or Millennium Development Goals. Paris.

▶ ORGANISATION FOR ECONOMIC CO-OPERATION AND DEVELOPMENT. DEVELOPMENT ASSISTANCE COMMITTEE (annual). *Development Co-operation Report*. Paris.

▶ ORGANISATION FOR ECONOMIC CO-OPERATION AND DEVELOPMENT. DEVELOPMENT ASSISTANCE COMMITTEE (annual). *International Development Statistics* CD-ROM. Paris.

▶ UNITED NATIONS (2003). *Millennium Indicators Database*. Statistics Division Internet site http://millenniumindicators.un.org .

AGENCY

Organisation for Economic Co-operation and Development/Development Assistance Committee

35 PROPORTION OF BILATERAL ODA OF OECD/DAC DONORS THAT IS UNTIED

DEFINITION

Official development assistance (ODA) comprises grants or loans to developing countries and territories on the OECD Development Assistance Committee list of aid recipients that are undertaken by the official sector with promotion of economic development and welfare as the main objective and at concessional financial terms (if a loan, having a grant element of at least 25 per cent). Technical cooperation is included. Grants, loans and credits for military purposes are excluded. Also excluded is aid to more advanced developing and transition countries as determined by the Committee. *Bilateral official development assistance* is from one country to another.

Untied bilateral official development assistance is assistance from country to country for which the associated goods and services may be fully and freely procured in substantially all countries.

GOAL AND TARGETS ADDRESSED

Goal 8. Develop a global partnership for development

Target 12. Develop further an open, rule-based, predictable, non-discriminatory trading and financial system. Includes a commitment to good governance, development and poverty reduction—both nationally and internationally

Target 13. Address the special needs of the least developed countries. Includes: tariff and quota-free access for least developed countries' exports; enhanced programme of debt relief for heavily indebted poor countries and cancellation of official bilateral debt; and more generous ODA for countries committed to poverty reduction

Target 14. Address the special needs of landlocked countries and small island developing States (through the Programme of Action for the Sustainable Development of Small Island Developing States and the outcome of the twenty-second special session of the General Assembly)

Target 15. Deal comprehensively with the debt problems of developing countries through national and international measures in order to make debt sustainable in the long term

RATIONALE

Tying procurement from aid contracts to suppliers in the donor country reduces its cost-

effectiveness. Recognizing this, OECD/DAC member countries have raised the share of their aid that is untied. The share of untied aid to the least developed countries has risen relatively slowly, but the situation is likely to improve with the implementation of the new DAC Recommendation on Untying Official Development Assistance to the Least Developed Countries.

DATA COLLECTION AND SOURCE

Data are compiled by the Development Assistance Committee of OECD.

PERIODICITY OF MEASUREMENT

Annual.

REFERENCES AND INTERNATIONAL DATA COMPARISONS

▶ ORGANISATION FOR ECONOMIC CO-OPERATION AND DEVELOPMENT. DEVELOPMENT ASSISTANCE COMMITTEE (2003). Internet site http://www.oecd.org/dac . Under Topics, select: Aid statistics, Aid effectiveness and donor practices or Millennium Development Goals. Paris.

▶ ORGANISATION FOR ECONOMIC CO-OPERATION AND DEVELOPMENT. DEVELOPMENT ASSISTANCE COMMITTEE (annual). *Development Co-operation Report*. Paris.

▶ ORGANISATION FOR ECONOMIC CO-OPERATION AND DEVELOPMENT. DEVELOPMENT ASSISTANCE COMMITTEE (annual). International Development Statistics. CD-ROM. Paris.

▶ UNITED NATIONS (2003). *Millennium Indicators Database*. Statistics Division Internet site http://millenniumindicators.un.org .

▶ UNITED NATIONS. OFFICE OF THE HIGH REPRESENTATIVE FOR THE LEAST DEVELOPED COUNTRIES, LANDLOCKED DEVELOPING COUNTRIES AND SMALL ISLAND DEVELOPING STATES (2003). Internet site http://www.un.org/ohrlls .

AGENCY

Organisation for Economic Co-operation and Development, Development Assistance Committee

36 ODA RECEIVED IN LANDLOCKED COUNTRIES AS PROPORTION OF THEIR GROSS NATIONAL INCOMES

DEFINITION

Official development assistance comprises grants or loans to developing countries and territories on the OECD Development Assistance Committee list of aid recipients that are undertaken by the official sector with promotion of economic development and welfare as the main objective and at concessional financial terms (if a loan, having a grant element of at least 25 per cent). Technical cooperation is included. Grants, loans and credits for military purposes are excluded. Also excluded is aid to more advanced developing and transition countries as determined by DAC.

Recipient countries' gross national income (GNI) at market prices is the sum of gross primary incomes receivable by resident institutional units and sectors. GNI at market prices was called gross national product (GNP) in the 1953 System of National Accounts. In contrast to gross domestic product (GDP), GNI is a concept of income (primary income) rather than value added.

The land-locked developing countries are, by region: *Africa*: Botswana, Burkina Faso, Burundi, the Central African Republic, Chad, Ethiopia, Lesotho, Malawi, Mali, Niger, Rwanda, Swaziland, Uganda, Zambia and Zimbabwe; *Asia and the Pacific*: Afghanistan, Azerbaijan, Bhutan, Kazakhstan, Kyrgyzstan, the Lao People's Democratic Republic, Mongolia, Nepal, Tajikistan, Turkmenistan and Uzbekistan; *Europe*: The former Yugoslav Republic of Macedonia and the Republic of Moldova (expected from 2003); *Latin America and the Caribbean*: Bolivia and Paraguay.

GOAL AND TARGETS ADDRESSED

Goal 8. Develop a global partnership for development

Target 12. Develop further an open, rule-based, predictable, non-discriminatory trading and financial system. Includes a commitment to good governance, development and poverty reduction—both nationally and internationally

Target 13:. Address the special needs of the least developed countries. Includes: tariff and quota-free access for least developed countries' exports; enhanced programme of debt relief for HIPCs and cancellation of official bilateral debt; and more generous ODA for countries committed to poverty reduction

Target 14. Address the special needs of landlocked countries and small island developing States (through the Programme of Action for the Sustainable Development of Small Island Developing States and the outcome of the twenty-second special session of the General Assembly)

Target 15. Deal comprehensively with the debt problems of developing countries through national and international measures in order to make debt sustainable in the long term

RATIONALE

The indicator addresses the special needs of landlocked countries to achieve their development goals.

DATA COLLECTION AND SOURCE

Data are compiled by the Development Assistance Committee of the Organisation for Economic Co-operation and Development

PERIODICITY OF MEASUREMENT

Annual.

REFERENCES AND INTERNATIONAL DATA COMPARISONS

▶ ORGANISATION FOR ECONOMIC CO-OPERATION AND DEVELOPMENT. DEVELOPMENT ASSISTANCE COMMITTEE (2003). Internet site http://www.oecd.org/dac. Under Topics, select: Aid statistics, Aid effectiveness and donor practices or Millennium Development Goals. Paris.

▶ ORGANISATION FOR ECONOMIC CO-OPERATION AND DEVELOPMENT. DEVELOPMENT ASSISTANCE COMMITTEE (annual). *Development Co-operation Report*. Paris.

▶ **ORGANISATION FOR ECONOMIC CO-OPERATION AND DEVELOPMENT. DEVELOPMENT ASSISTANCE COMMITTEE** (annual). *International Development Statistics*. CD-ROM. Paris.

▶ **UNITED NATIONS** (2003). *Millennium Indicators Database*. Statistics Division Internet site http://millenniumindicators.un.org.

▶ **UNITED NATIONS, COMMISSION OF THE EUROPEAN COMMUNITIES, INTERNATIONAL MONETARY FUND, ORGANISATION FOR ECONOMIC CO-OPERATION AND DEVELOPMENT** and **WORLD BANK** (1994). *System of National Accounts 1993 (SNA 1993)*, Series F, No.2, Rev. 4. Sales No. E.94.XVII.4. Available with updates at http://unstats.un.org/unsd/sna1993.

▶ **UNITED NATIONS. OFFICE OF THE HIGH REPRESENTATIVE FOR THE LEAST DEVELOPED COUNTRIES, LANDLOCKED DEVELOPING COUNTRIES AND SMALL ISLAND DEVELOPING STATES** (2003). Internet site http://www.un.org/ohrlls.

AGENCY

Organisation for Economic Co-operation and Development/Development Assistance Committee.

37 ODA RECEIVED IN SMALL ISLAND DEVELOPING STATES AS PROPORTION OF THEIR GROSS NATIONAL INCOMES

DEFINITION

Official development assistance comprises grants or loans to developing countries and territories on the OECD Development Assistance Committee list of aid recipients that are undertaken by the official sector with promotion of economic development and welfare as the main objective and at concessional financial terms (if a loan, having a grant element of at least 25 per cent). Technical cooperation is included. Grants, loans and credits for military purposes are excluded. Also excluded is aid to more advanced developing and transition countries as determined by DAC.

Recipient countries' gross national income at market prices is the sum of gross primary incomes receivable by resident institutional units and sectors. GNI at market prices was called gross national product in the 1953 System of National Accounts. In contrast to gross domestic product, GNI is a concept of income (primary income) rather than value added.

The small island developing States are by region: *Africa*: Cape Verde, Comoros, Guinea-Bissau, Mauritius, Saõ Tomé and Principe, and Seychelles; *Asia and the Pacific*: Bahrain, Cook Islands, Fiji, Kiribati, Maldives, Marshall Islands, Micronesia (Federated States of), Nauru, Niue, Palau, Papua New Guinea, Samoa, Singapore, Solomon Islands, Timor Leste, Tokelau, Tonga, Tuvalu and Vanuatu; *Europe*: Cyprus and Malta; *Latin America and the Caribbean*: Antigua and Barbuda, Aruba, the Bahamas, Barbados, Belize, Cuba, Dominica, the Dominican Republic, Grenada, Guyana, Haiti, Jamaica, Netherlands Antilles, St. Kitts and Nevis, St. Lucia, St. Vincent and the Grenadines, Suriname, Trinidad and Tobago, and the U.S. Virgin Islands.

GOAL AND TARGETS ADDRESSED

Goal 8. Develop a global partnership for development

Target 12. Develop further an open, rule-based, predictable, non-discriminatory trading and financial system. Includes a commitment to good governance, development and poverty reduction—both nationally and internationally

Target 13. Address the special needs of the least developed countries. Includes: tariff and quota-free access for least developed countries' exports; enhanced programme of debt relief for heavily indebted poor countries and cancellation of official bilateral debt; and more generous ODA for countries committed to poverty reduction

Target 14. Address the special needs of landlocked countries and small island developing States (through the Programme of Action for the Sustainable Development of Small Island Developing States and the outcome of the twenty-second special session of the General Assembly)

Target 15. Deal comprehensively with the debt problems of developing countries through national and international measures in order to make debt sustainable in the long term

RATIONALE

The indicator addresses the special needs of small island developing States. That group of countries has very diverse incomes per capita, ranging from the least developed countries to high-income countries. The least developed countries need continued aid, which should be monitored closely.

DATA COLLECTION AND SOURCE

Data are compiled by the Development Assistance Committee of OECD.

PERIODICITY OF MEASUREMENT

Annual.

REFERENCES AND INTERNATIONAL DATA COMPARISONS

▸ ORGANISATION FOR ECONOMIC CO-OPERATION AND DEVELOPMENT. DEVELOPMENT ASSISTANCE COMMITTEE (2003). Internet site http://www.oecd.org/ dac. Under Topics, select: Aid statistics, Aid effectiveness and donor practices or Millennium Development Goals. Paris.

▸ ORGANISATION FOR ECONOMIC CO-OPERATION AND DEVELOPMENT. DEVELOPMENT ASSISTANCE COMMITTEE (annual). *Development Co-operation Report*. Paris.

▸ ORGANISATION FOR ECONOMIC CO-OPERATION AND DEVELOPMENT. DEVELOPMENT ASSISTANCE COMMITTEE (annual). *International Development Statistics*. CD-ROM. Paris.

▸ UNITED NATIONS (2003). *Millennium Indicators Database*. Statistics Division Internet site http://millenniumindicators.un.org.

▸ UNITED NATIONS, COMMISSION OF THE EUROPEAN COMMUNITIES, INTERNATIONAL MONETARY FUND, ORGANISATION FOR ECONOMIC CO-OPERATION AND

DEVELOPMENT and WORLD BANK (1994). *System of National Accounts 1993 (SNA 1993)*, Series F, No.2, Rev. 4. Sales No. E.94.XVII.4. Available with updates from http://unstats.un.org/ unsd/sna1993.

▸ UNITED NATIONS. OFFICE OF THE HIGH REPRESENTATIVE FOR THE LEAST DEVELOPED COUNTRIES, LANDLOCKED DEVELOPING COUNTRIES AND SMALL ISLAND DEVELOPING STATES (2003). Internet site http://www.un.org/ohrlls.

AGENCY

Organisation for Economic Co-operation and Development/Development Assistance Committee

38 **PROPORTION OF TOTAL DEVELOPED COUNTRY IMPORTS (BY VALUE AND EXCLUDING ARMS) FROM DEVELOPING COUNTRIES AND FROM THE LEASE DEVELOPED COUNTRIES, ADMITTED FREE OF DUTY**

DEFINITION

Imports and imported value of goods (merchandise) are goods that add to the stock of material resources of a country by entering its economic territory. Goods simply being transported through a country (goods in transit) or temporarily admitted (except for goods for inward processing) do not add to the stock of material resources of a country and are not included in international merchandise trade statistics. In many cases, a country's economic territory largely coincides with its customs territory, which is the territory in which the customs laws of a country apply in full.

Goods admitted free of duties are exports of goods (excluding arms) received from developing countries and admitted without tariffs to developed countries.

There is no established convention for the designation of *developed* and *developing* countries or areas in the United Nations system.

In common practice, Japan in Asia, Canada and the United States in North America, Australia and New Zealand in Oceania and Europe are considered "developed" regions or areas. In international trade statistics, the Southern African Customs Union is also treated as a developed region, and Israel is treated as a developed country; countries emerging from the former Yugoslavia are treated as developing countries; and countries of eastern Europe and European countries of the former Soviet Union are not included under either developed or developing regions.

The General Assembly, on the recommendation of the Committee for Development Policy, through the Economic and Social Council decides on the countries to be included in the list of *least developed countries* (LDCs). As of January 2004, the list included the following countries, by region: *Africa*: Angola, Benin, Burkina Faso, Burundi, Cape Verde, the Central African Republic, Chad, Comoros, the Democratic Republic of the Congo, Djibouti, Equatorial Guinea, Eritrea, Ethiopia, the Gambia, Guinea, Guinea-Bissau, Lesotho, Liberia, Madagascar, Malawi, Mali, Mauritania, Mozambique, Niger, Rwanda, Saõ Tomé and Principe, Senegal, Sierra Leone, Somalia, the Sudan, Togo, Uganda, the United Republic of Tanzania and Zambia; *Asia and the Pacific*: Afghanistan, Bangladesh, Bhutan, Cambodia, Kiribati, the Lao People's Democratic Republic., Maldives, Myanmar, Nepal, Samoa, Solomon Islands, Timor Leste, Tuvalu, Vanuatu and Yemen; *Latin America and the Caribbean*: Haiti.

GOAL AND TARGETS ADDRESSED

Goal 8:. Develop a global partnership for development

Target 12. Develop further an open, rule-based, predictable, non-discriminatory trading and financial system. Includes a commitment to good governance, development and poverty reduction—both nationally and internationally

Target 13. Address the special needs of the least developed countries. Includes: tariff and quota-free access for least developed countries' exports; enhanced programme of debt relief for heavily indebted poor countries and cancellation of official bilateral debt; and more generous ODA for countries committed to poverty reduction

Target 14. Address the special needs of land-locked countries and small island developing States (through the Programme of Action for the Sustainable Development of Small Island Developing States and the outcome of the twenty-second special session of the General Assembly)

Target 15. Deal comprehensively with the debt problems of developing countries through national and international measures in order to make debt sustainable in the long term

RATIONALE

The indicator monitors the international effort made to remove barriers to trade for developing countries, to encourage the achievement of the Millennium Development Goals. Poor people in developing countries work primarily in agriculture and labour-intensive manufacturing, sectors that confront the greatest trade barriers. Removing barriers to merchandise trade, therefore, could increase growth in those countries by a significant amount.

METHOD OF COMPUTATION

To value their exports, countries can choose free-on-board (f.o.b.) values, which include only the transaction value of the goods and the value of services performed to deliver goods to the border of the exporting country, or cost, insurance and freight (c.i.f.) values, which add to this the value of the services performed to deliver the goods from the border of the exporting country to the border of the importing country. It is recommended that imported goods be valued at c.i.f. prices for statistical purposes. Specific duties—not expressed as a proportion of the declared value—may or may not be included in calculations of goods admitted free of duties.

DATA COLLECTION AND SOURCE

The indicator is calculated by the United Nations Conference on Trade and Development in collaboration with the World Bank and the World Trade Organization, from the Trade Analysis and Information System (TRAINS) CD-ROM, version 8 (2002).

COMMENTS AND LIMITATIONS

Indicator data available only at the world level.

REFERENCES AND INTERNATIONAL DATA COMPARISONS

▶ UNITED NATIONS (1998). *International Merchandise Trade Statistics – Concepts and Definitions*, Series M, No. 52, Rev. 2. Sales No. E.98.XVII.16. Available from http:// unstats.un.org/unsd/pubs (A, C, E, F, R, S).

▶ UNITED NATIONS (2003). *Millennium Indicators Database*. Statistics Division Internet site http://millenniumindicators.un.org.

▶ UNITED NATIONS, COMMISSION OF THE EUROPEAN COMMUNITIES, INTERNATIONAL MONETARY FUND, ORGANISATION FOR ECONOMIC CO-OPERATION AND DEVELOPMENT and WORLD BANK (1994). *System of National Accounts 1993 (SNA 1993)*, Series F, No.2, Rev. 4. Sales No. E.94.XVII.4, para. 7.66 for import duties. Available with updates at http://unstats. un.org/unsd/sna 1993.

▶ UNITED NATIONS CONFERENCE ON TRADE AND DEVELOPMENT (2003). *Trade Analysis and Information System (TRAINS)*. Internet site http://r0.unctad.org/trains. Geneva.

▶ UNITED NATIONS. OFFICE OF THE HIGH REPRESENTATIVE FOR THE LEAST DEVELOPED COUNTRIES, LANDLOCKED DEVELOPING COUNTRIES AND SMALL ISLAND DEVELOPING STATES (2003). Internet site http://www.un.org/ohrlls.

▶ WORLD CUSTOMS ORGANIZATION (1996). *Harmonized Commodity Description and Coding Systems, Second Edition (HS)*. Brussels. English, French.

Data discrepancies across countries limit international comparison.

AGENCY

World Trade Organization.

39 AVERAGE TARIFFS IMPOSED BY DEVELOPED COUNTRIES ON AGRICULTURAL PRODUCTS AND CLOTHING FROM DEVELOPING COUNTRIES

DEFINITION

Average tariffs are the simple average of all applied ad valorem tariffs (tariffs based on the value of the import) applicable to the bilateral imports of developed countries. *Agricultural products* comprise plant and animal products, including tree crops but excluding timber and fish products. *Clothing* and textiles include natural and synthetic fibers and fabrics and articles of clothing made from them.

GOAL AND TARGETS ADDRESSED

Goal 8. Develop a global partnership for development

Target 12. Develop further an open, rule-based, predictable, non-discriminatory trading and financial system. Includes a commitment to good governance, development and poverty reduction—both nationally and internationally

Target 13. Address the special needs of the least developed countries. Includes: tariff and quota-free access for least developed countries' exports; enhanced programme of debt relief for heavily indebted poor countries and cancellation of official bilateral debt; and more generous ODA for countries committed to poverty reduction

Target 14. Address the special needs of land-locked countries and small island developing States (through the Programme of Action for the Sustainable Development of Small Island Developing States and the outcome of the twenty-second special session of the General Assembly)

Target 15. Deal comprehensively with the debt problems of developing countries through national and international measures in order to make debt sustainable in the long term

RATIONALE

The indicator monitors the international effort made to remove barriers to trade for developing countries in order to encourage the achievement of the Millennium Development Goals. Poor people in developing countries work primarily in agriculture and labour-intensive manufacturing, sectors that confront the greatest trade barriers. Removing barriers to merchandise trade, therefore, could increase growth in those countries by a significant amount.

METHOD OF COMPUTATION

To calculate average tariffs, each Harmonized System six-digit bilateral trade flow is given the same weight. The results for each developed country are then aggregated using the standard import pattern as the weighting scheme for all importers. The standard weighting scheme would be the average import structure of all developed markets for imports from the least developed countries and from developing countries. The tariff rates used are the available ad valorem rates, including most-favoured nation and non-most-favoured-nation (largely preferential) rates. As it is not possible to convert non-ad valorem rates to ad valorem equivalents, all tariff lines with non-ad valorem rates are excluded from the calculation. This affects, in particular, agricultural products, where almost 25 per cent of the Harmonized System six-digit product categories contain at least one non-ad valorem tariff line. Therefore, the agricultural part of the indicator is excluded from the initial data set until an appropriate methodology for treating non-ad valorem tariffs is developed.

DATA COLLECTION AND SOURCE

The indicator is calculated by the United Nations Conference on Trade and Development and the World Trade Organization in consultation with the World Bank from the Trade Analysis and Information System (TRAINS) CD-ROM, version 8 (2002). Organisation for Economic Co-operation and Development database, www.oecd.org. *Agricultural Market Access Database*, http://www.amad.org.

COMMENTS AND LIMITATIONS

There are two types of average tariffs—simple average tariffs, which are used for goals monitoring, and the weighted average. Simple averages are frequently a better indicator of tariff protection than weighted averages, which, because higher tariffs discourage trade and reduce the weights applied to them, are biased downward .

REFERENCES AND INTERNATIONAL DATA COMPARISONS

▸ UNITED NATIONS (1998). *International Merchandise Trade Statistics – Concepts and Definitions*, Series M, No. 52, Rev. 2. Sales No. E.98.XVII.16. Available from http://unstats.un.org/unsd/pubs (A, C, E, F, R, S).

▸ UNITED NATIONS (2003). *Millennium Indicators Database*. Statistics Division Internet site http://millenniumindicators.un.org.

▸ WORLD CUSTOMS ORGANIZATION (1996). *Harmonized Commodity Description and Coding System* (HS), Second Edition. Brussels. English, French.

Data discrepancies across countries limit international comparison.

AGENCY

World Trade Organization

40 AGRICULTURAL SUPPORT ESTIMATE FOR OECD COUNTRIES AS A PERCENTAGE OF THEIR GROSS DOMESTIC PRODUCT

DEFINITION

Agricultural support is the annual monetary value of all gross transfers from taxpayers and consumers, both domestic and foreign (in the form of subsidies arising from policy measures that support agriculture), net of the associated budgetary receipts, regardless of their objectives and impacts on farm production and income, or consumption of farm products.

For agricultural products, the total support estimate represents the overall taxpayer and consumer costs of agricultural policies. When expressed as a *percentage of GDP*, the total support estimate is an indicator of the cost to the economy as a whole.

GOAL AND TARGETS ADDRESSED

Goal 8. Develop a global partnership for development

Target 12. Develop further an open, rule-based, predictable, non-discriminatory trading and financial system. Includes a commitment to good governance, development and poverty reduction—both nationally and internationally

Target 13. Address the special needs of the least developed countries. Includes: tariff and quota-free access for least developed countries' exports; enhanced programme of debt relief for heavily indebted poor countries and cancellation of official bilateral debt; and more generous ODA for countries committed to poverty reduction

Target 14. Address the special needs of land-locked countries and small island developing States (through the Programme of Action for the Sustainable Development of Small Island Developing States and the outcome of the twenty-second special session of the General Assembly)

Target 15. Deal comprehensively with the debt problems of developing countries through national and international measures in order to make debt sustainable in the long term

RATIONALE

In penetrating foreign markets, developing countries face not only tariffs but also competition from products in developed countries that benefit from government subsidies. The challenge linked to the Doha Development Agenda is to further reduce production and trade-distorting support and implement policies that effectively address both domestic and international

goals while ensuring well-functioning markets.

METHOD OF COMPUTATION

The agricultural total support estimate includes support to individual farmers from trade barriers that keep domestic farm prices above those on world markets, budget-financed payments, input subsidies, consumer food subsidies and support to general services provided to the agricultural sector as a whole.

PERIODICITY OF MEASUREMENT

Annual.

COMMENTS AND LIMITATIONS

Differences across countries in total support estimates as a percentage of GDP reflect the level of support and the share of agricultural output in the economy. Changes over time reflect changes in the level of support and in the share of agriculture in GDP, as well as the growth of the economy.

REFERENCES AND INTERNATIONAL DATA COMPARISONS

▸ ORGANISATION FOR ECONOMIC CO-OPERATION AND DEVELOPMENT (2003). Producer and Consumer Support Estimates, OECD Database 1986-2002, User's Guide. Paris. Available from http://www.oecd.org/dataoecd/47/20/43 51287.pdf.

▸ ORGANISATION FOR ECONOMIC CO-OPERATION AND DEVELOPMENT (2003). *Producer and Consumer Support Estimates, OECD Database 1986-2002.* Internet site http://www.oecd.org, Select Statistics/Agriculture and Fisheries. Paris.

▸ ORGANISATION FOR ECONOMIC CO-OPERATION AND DEVELOPMENT (annual). *Agricultural Policies in OECD Countries, Monitoring and Evaluation.* Paris.

▸ UNITED NATIONS (2003). *Millennium Indicators Database.* Statistics Division Internet site *http://millenniumindicators.un.org.*

▸ UNITED NATIONS, COMMISSION OF THE EUROPEAN COMMUNITIES, INTERNATIONAL MONETARY FUND, ORGANISATION FOR ECONOMIC CO-OPERATION AND DEVELOPMENT and WORLD BANK (1994).

System of National Accounts 1993 (SNA 1993), Series F, No.2, Rev. 4. Sales No. E.94.XVII.4. Available with updates from http://unstats.un.org/unsd/sna1993.

AGENCY
Organisation for Economic Co-operation and Development

41 PROPORTION OF ODA PROVIDED TO HELP BUILD TRADE CAPACITY

DEFINITION
Official development assistance comprises grants or loans to developing countries and territories on the OECD Development Assistance Committee list of aid recipients that are undertaken by the official sector with promotion of economic development and welfare as the main objective and at concessional financial terms (if a loan, having a grant element of at least 25 per cent). Technical cooperation is included. Grants, loans and credits for military purposes are excluded. Also excluded is aid to more advanced developing and transition countries as determined by DAC.

Activities to *help build trade capacity* enhance the ability of the recipient country
- To formulate and implement a trade development strategy and create an enabling environment for increasing the volume and value-added of exports, diversifying export products and markets and increasing foreign investment to generate jobs and trade
- To stimulate trade by domestic firms and encourage investment in trade-oriented industries
- To participate in the benefit from the institutions, negotiations and processes that shape national trade policy and the rules and practices of international commerce

Those activities are further classified by the *First Joint WTO/OECD Report on Trade-Related Technical Assistance and Capacity-Building* (2002) under two main categories, trade policy and regulations (divided into nineteen subcategories) and trade development (divided into six subcategories).

GOAL AND TARGETS ADDRESSED
Goal 8. Develop a global partnership for development
Target 12. Develop further an open, rule-based, predictable, non-discriminatory trading and financial system. Includes a commitment to good governance, development and poverty reduction—both nationally and internationally
Target 13. Address the special needs of the least developed countries. Includes: tariff and quota-free access for least developed countries' exports; enhanced programme of debt relief for heavily indebted poor countries and cancellation of official bilateral debt; and more generous ODA for countries committed to poverty reduction
Target 14. Address the special needs of landlocked countries and small island developing States (through the Programme of Action for the Sustainable Development of Small Island Developing States and the outcome of the twenty-second special session of the General Assembly)
Target 15. Deal comprehensively with the debt problems of developing countries through national and international measures in order to make debt sustainable in the long term

RATIONALE
At the Fourth Ministerial Conference of the World Trade Organization, held in Doha in 2001, donors committed to providing increased support to help developing countries, especially the least developed countries, build the capacity to trade and to integrate into world markets.

Data collected for the indicator will help monitor the following aspects of trade-related official development assistance:

- Transparency of trade-related technical assistance delivered
- Sharing of information
- Minimization and avoidance of duplication
- Estimation of progress in the implementation of the Doha mandates on technical cooperation and capacity-building
- Coordination and coherence
- Achievement of the objectives mandated in paragraph 41 of the Ministerial Declaration adopted by the Conference at Doha

METHOD OF COMPUTATION
See "Comments and limitations".

DATA COLLECTION AND SOURCE
The World Trade Organization and the OECD have compiled the *Doha Development Agenda Trade Capacity-Building Database* (TCBDB) that lists and quantify activities by bilateral and multilateral donors from 2001 onwards. The database lists both the number and the value of activities.

Data are reported from bilateral donors and multilateral and regional agencies that replied to the requests for information sent in May 2002 and April 2003 by the director-general of the World Trade Organization and the secretary-general of the Organisation for Economic Co-operation and Development.

COMMENTS AND LIMITATIONS
Donors differ in defining what constitutes a single "activity". Some donors split individual activities into components in order to obtain detailed data on aid allocated to each subcategory. Others classify the whole activity under the most relevant subcategory. For some donors, the number of records in the database is larger than the actual number of activities. In the Joint Report by the World Trade Organization and the Organisation for Economic Co-operation and Development, the data are based on the actual number of activities.

There are also differences in the methodology used for reporting trade development activities among donors who replied to the requests for information. A number of donors isolated the trade components of each activity, whereas others reported the whole activity as trade related. The total amounts of trade-related technical assistance and capacity building per donor in this category should therefore be interpreted with caution.

The joint report also highlights the need to refine the activity categories to better identify general trade development activities, such as trade fairs, trade information, publications or general export training. At present, most of those activities appear under "business support services and institutions".

These issues are being addressed in the first update to the data, with results online by August 2003.

REFERENCES AND INTERNATIONAL DATA COMPARISONS

▸ ORGANISATION FOR ECONOMIC CO-OPERATION AND DEVELOPMENT. DEVELOPMENT ASSISTANCE COMMITTEE (2003). Internet site http://www.oecd.org/dac. Under topics, select: Aid statistics, Aid effectiveness and donor practices or Millennium Development Goals. Paris.

▸ ORGANISATION FOR ECONOMIC CO-OPERATION AND DEVELOPMENT. DEVELOPMENT ASSISTANCE COMMITTEE (annual). *Development Co-operation Report*. Paris.

▸ ORGANISATION FOR ECONOMIC CO-OPERATION AND DEVELOPMENT. DEVELOPMENT ASSISTANCE COMMITTEE (annual). *International Development Statistics* CD-ROM. Paris.

▸ WORLD TRADE ORGANIZATION AND ORGANISATION FOR ECONOMIC CO-OPERATION AND DEVELOPMENT (2003 and annual). *Joint WTO/OECD Report on Trade-Related Technical Assistance and Capacity-Building*, Management of Trade Capacity-Building. Paris and Geneva. Available from http://tcbdb.wto.org/stat-analysis.asp.

AGENCIES
Organisation for Economic Co-operation and Development
World Trade Organization

42 TOTAL NUMBER OF COUNTRIES THAT HAVE REACHED THEIR HIPC DECISION POINTS AND NUMBER THAT HAVE REACHED THEIR HIPC COMPLETION POINTS (CUMULATIVE)

DEFINITION
The HIPC decision point is the date at which a heavily indebted poor country with an established track record of good performance under adjustment programmes supported by the International Monetary Fund (IMF) and the World Bank commits to undertake additional reforms and to develop and implement a poverty reduction strategy.

The HIPC completion point is the date at which the country successfully completes the key structural reforms agreed at the decision point, including the development and implementation of its poverty reduction strategy. The country then receives the bulk of debt relief under the HIPC Initiative without any further policy conditions.

GOAL AND TARGETS ADDRESSED
Goal 8. Develop a global partnership for development
Target 12. Develop further an open, rule-based, predictable, non-discriminatory trading and financial system. Includes a commitment to good governance, development and poverty reduction—both nationally and internationally
Target 13. Address the special needs of the least developed countries. Includes: tariff and quota-free access for least developed countries' exports; enhanced programme of debt relief for heavily indebted poor countries and cancellation of official bilateral debt; and more generous ODA for countries committed to poverty reduction
Target 14. Address the special needs of landlocked countries and small island developing States (through the Programme of Action for the Sustainable Development of Small Island Developing States and the outcome of the twenty-second special session of the General Assembly)
Target 15. Deal comprehensively with the debt problems of developing countries through national and international measures in order to make debt sustainable in the long term

RATIONALE
A global partnership for development requires increased debt reduction for heavily indebted poor countries. The indicator will monitor the Heavily Indebted Poor Countries Initiative, a major international effort targeted specifically at improving developing countries' debt sustainability. Launched in 1996 and enhanced in 1999 to broaden and accelerate debt relief, the HIPC Initiative marked the first time that multilateral, official bilateral and commercial creditors united in a joint effort to reduce the external debt of the world's most debt-laden poor countries to sustainable levels.

METHOD OF COMPUTATION
See "Definition".

DATA COLLECTION AND SOURCE
Information is compiled by the IMF and World Bank from their HIPC decision and completion point documents (see "References").

PERIODICITY OF MEASUREMENT
Twice a year.

COMMENTS AND LIMITATIONS
The Heavily Indebted Poor Countries Initiative was launched in 1996. The earliest available data are for 2000 and the most recent available data are for 2002.

REFERENCES AND INTERNATIONAL DATA
COMPARISONS

▶ **INTERNATIONAL MONETARY FUND** (2003). *Debt Relief under the Heavily Indebted Poor Countries (HIPC) Initiative*. Internet site http://www.imf.org/external/np/exr/facts/hipc.htm. Washington, D.C.

▶ **UNITED NATIONS** (2003). *Millennium Indicators Database*. Statistics Division Internet site http://millenniumindicators.un.org.

World Bank, www.worldbank.org/hipc.

AGENCIES
International Monetary Fund
World Bank

43 DEBT RELIEF COMMITTED UNDER HIPC INITIATIVE

DEFINITION
Debt relief committed under HIPC Initiative (in United States dollars) as a component of official development assistance has been recorded in different ways over time. Up through 1992, forgiveness of non-official development assistance debt that met the tests of official development assistance was reportable as ODA. During 1990–1992 it remained reportable as part of a country's ODA, but was excluded from the Development Assistance Committee total. Since 1993, forgiveness of debt originally intended for military purposes has been reportable as "other official flows", while forgiveness of other non-ODA loans (mainly export credits) recorded as ODA has been included in both country data and total Committee ODA, as it was until 1989.

GOAL AND TARGETS ADDRESSED
Goal 8. Develop a global partnership for development
Target 12. Develop further an open, rule-based, predictable, non-discriminatory trading and financial system. Includes a commitment to good governance, development and poverty reduction—both nationally and internationally
Target 13. Address the special needs of the least developed countries. Includes: tariff and quota-free access for least developed countries' exports; enhanced programme of debt relief for heavily indebted poor countries and cancellation of official bilateral debt; and more generous ODA for countries committed to poverty reduction
Target 14. Address the special needs of land-locked countries and small island developing States (through the Programme of Action for the Sustainable Development of Small Island Developing States and the outcome of the twenty-second special session of the General Assembly)
Target 15. Deal comprehensively with the debt problems of developing countries through national and international measures in order to make debt sustainable in the long term

RATIONALE
A global partnership for development requires increased debt reduction for heavily indebted poor countries. The indicator will monitor the Heavily Indebted Poor Countries Initiative, a major international effort targeted specifically at improving developing countries' debt sustainability. Launched in 1996 and enhanced in 1999 to broaden and accelerate debt relief, the HIPC Initiative marked the first time that multilateral, official bilateral and commercial creditors united in a joint effort to reduce the external debt of the world's most debt-laden poor countries to sustainable levels.

METHOD OF COMPUTATION
See "Definition" and *The DAC Journal: Development Cooperation Report* and the OECD/DAC *International Development Statistics* CD-ROM for notes on definitions.

DATA COLLECTION AND SOURCE
Information is compiled by the International Monetary Fund and the World Bank from their HIPC decision and completion point docu-

ments (see "References").

PERIODICITY OF MEASUREMENT
Annual.

DISAGGREGATION ISSUES
Figures are available by country.

REFERENCES AND INTERNATIONAL DATA COMPARISONS

▶ INTERNATIONAL MONETARY FUND (2003). *Debt Relief under the Heavily Indebted Poor Countries (HIPC) Initiative.* Internet site http://www.imf.org/external/np/exr/facts /hipc.htm. Washington, D.C.

▶ UNITED NATIONS (2003). *Millennium Indicators Database.* Statistics Division Internet site http://millenniumindicators.un.org.

▶ WORLD BANK (2003 and annual). *World Development Indicators.* Print and CD-ROM. Washington, D.C. Available in part from http://www.worldbank.org/data.

▶ WORLD BANK (2003). *Debt Initiative for the Heavily Indebted Poor Countries (HIPCs).* Internet site http://www.worldbank.org/hipc. Washington, D.C.

AGENCIES
International Monetary Fund
World Bank

44 DEBT SERVICE AS A PERCENTAGE OF EXPORTS OF GOODS AND SERVICES

DEFINITION
External debt service refers to principal repayments and interest payments made to non-residents in foreign currency, goods or services. Long-term refers to debt that has an original or extended maturity of more than one year.

Exports of goods and services comprise sales, barter or gifts or grants of goods and services from residents to non-residents. Where exports of goods are valued f.o.b., the costs of transportation and insurance up to the border of the exporting country are included in exports of goods. Other transactions involving a mixture of goods and services, such as expenditures by foreign travellers in the domestic market, may all have to be recorded under services in the rest of the world account. Export receipts along with worker remittances received from abroad provide the foreign exchange proceeds for meeting external debt service obligations.

GOAL AND TARGETS ADDRESSED
Goal 8. Develop a global partnership for development

Target 12. Develop further an open, rule-based, predictable, non-discriminatory trading and financial system. Includes a commitment to good governance, development and poverty reduction—both nationally and internationally

Target 13. Address the special needs of the least developed countries. Includes: tariff and quota-free access for least developed countries' exports; enhanced programme of debt relief for HIPCs and cancellation of official bilateral debt; and more generous ODA for countries committed to poverty reduction

Target 14. Address the special needs of landlocked countries and small island developing States (through the Programme of Action for the Sustainable Development of Small Island Developing States and the outcome of the twenty-second special session of the General Assembly)

Target 15. Deal comprehensively with the debt problems of developing countries through national and international measures in order to make debt sustainable in the long term

RATIONALE
The targets on debt relief also address the need to make debt sustainable in the long term. The indicator is one measure of whether debt levels are sustainable.

METHOD OF COMPUTATION
The indicator is calculated as the ratio of external debt service to exports of goods and services, expressed as a percentage.

DATA COLLECTION AND SOURCE
The World Bank collects data on indicators of finance, published annually in *Global*

Development Finance.

PERIODICITY OF MEASUREMENT
Annual.

COMMENTS AND LIMITATIONS
Small, open economies may have relatively high levels of exports (and imports) and yet may face problems in meeting debt service obligations, particularly when debt service payments due on public debt are high relative to government revenue. A large economy may have proportionately smaller exports and still find its dept payments sustainable. For this reason, it is useful to look at other indicators, such as the ratio of total debt to gross national income, the size of international reserves relative to total debt and debt maturing within a year's time, in forming a picture of debt sustainability.

REFERENCES AND INTERNATIONAL DATA COMPARISONS
▸ **INTERNATIONAL MONETARY FUND** (2003). *Debt Relief under the Heavily Indebted Poor Countries (HIPC) Initiative*. Internet site http://www.imf.org/external/np/exr/facts/hipc.htm. Washington, D.C.

▸ **UNITED NATIONS** (1998). *International Merchandise Trade Statistics – Concepts and Definitions*, Series M, No. 52, Rev. 2. Sales No.E.98.XVII.16. Available from http://unstats.un.org/unsd/pubs (A, C, E, F, R, S).

▸ **UNITED NATIONS** (2003). *Millennium Indicators Database*. Statistics Division Internet site http://millenniumindicators.un.org.

▸ **UNITED NATIONS, COMMISSION OF THE EUROPEAN COMMUNITIES, INTERNATIONAL MONETARY FUND, ORGANISATION FOR ECONOMIC CO-OPERATION AND DEVELOPMENT** and **WORLD BANK** (1994). *System of National Accounts 1993 (SNA 1993)*, Series F, No.2, Rev. 4. Sales No. E.94.XVII.4. Available with updates from http://unstats.un.org/unsd/sna1993.

▸ **WORLD BANK** (2003). *Debt Initiative for the Heavily Indebted Poor Countries (HIPCs)*. Internet site http://www.worldbank.org/hipc. Washington, D.C.

▸ **WORLD BANK** (annual). *Global Development Finance*, vol. 2, Country Tables. Washington, D.C.

AGENCIES
International Monetary Fund
World Bank

 45 UNEMPLOYMENT RATE OF YOUNG PEOPLE AGED 15–24 YEARS, EACH SEX AND TOTAL

DEFINITION
*Unemployment rate of young people aged 15–24 year*s is the number of unemployed people ages 15–24 divided by the labour force of the same age group. *Unemployed people* are all those who are not employed during a specified reference period but are available for work and have taken concrete steps to seek paid employment or self-employment. In situations where the conventional means of seeking work are of limited relevance, where the labour market is largely unorganized or of limited scope, where labour absorption is temporarily inadequate or where the labour force is largely self-employed, a relaxed definition of unemployment can be applied, based on only the first two criteria (without work and currently available for work).

The *labour force* consists of those who are employed plus those who are unemployed during the relevant reference period. It is the economically active portion of the population. *Employment* refers to being engaged in an economic activity during a specified reference period or being temporarily absent from such an activity, while *economic activity* refers to the production of goods and services for pay or profit or for use by own household.

GOAL AND TARGET ADDRESSED
Goal 8. Develop a global partnership for development
Target 16. In cooperation with developing

countries, develop and implement strategies for decent and productive work for youth

RATIONALE

The indicator monitors the degree to which the youth labour force is utilized in the economy and therefore serves as a measure of the success of strategies to create jobs for youth.

METHOD OF COMPUTATION

The number of people aged 15–24 years who are unemployed is divided by the number of people in the labour force of the same age group.

DATA COLLECTION AND SOURCE

Country data are available from labour force surveys, administrative records, official national estimates and population censuses. Labour force surveys generally provide the most comprehensive and comparable source of information. Concepts and definitions adopted for data collection in labour force surveys also generally conform to International Labour Organization (ILO) resolutions and recommendations, such as the International Conference of Labour Statisticians resolution on international standards for unemployment and youth unemployment.

PERIODICITY OF MEASUREMENT

Results from population censuses are normally available every 10 years. Labour force surveys may be available annually or even more frequently in OECD countries and generally every three to five years in developing countries

GENDER ISSUES

Female unemployment rates are often significantly higher than male unemployment rates. However, unemployment data do not adequately reflect the situation of women in the labour market, especially in developing countries where women are engaged in subsistence work and, more often than men, work in the informal sector. In those settings, women are seldom employed, although they may often be underemployed. Furthermore, women may not have easy access to formal channels for seeking employment, particularly in rural areas, and often face social and cultural barriers when looking for a job. Thus official labour statistics may undercount women's unemployment (unless the relaxed definition of unemployment is used and adequate criteria are adopted in data collection).

DISAGGREGATION ISSUES

In most countries, data are available separately for men and women.

INTERNATIONAL DATA COMPILATIONS

ILO compiles internationally comparable data series on unemployment and youth unemployment.

▸ *Bulletin of Labour Statistics*, 2002–4. International Labour Organization. Geneva.
▸ *Key Indicators of the Labour Market* (annual). International Labour Organization. Available in part from http://www.ilo.org/kilm.

COMMENTS AND LIMITATIONS

The concepts of *employment* and *unemployment* have different relevance depending on the level of labour market development and the presence of a market economy. People living in regions of a country where there is little or no formal employment would not usually be classified as "unemployed" even if they are without work and would accept a job if offered one (discouraged workers).

Unemployment is but one dimension of the employment problem faced by young people. A disproportionately large number of youth in many countries are underemployed. Some work fewer hours than they would like to, and others work long hours with little economic gain. Stagnation and decline of employment opportunities in the formal sector of most developing countries have intensified the problem in recent years, with young women bearing a disproportionate share of the burden. Therefore, indicators measuring underemployment, the informal sector, educational access and labour force participation, among others, should supplement the information obtained from the youth unemployment indicator.

Limitations to comparability arise from various causes, including different sources, measurement methodologies, number of observations per year and coverage. Comparability may also be limited by conceptual variations, involving issues such as the definition of job search or whether to include discouraged workers who are not currently looking for work.

REFERENCES AND INTERNATIONAL DATA COMPARISONS

▸ **INTERNATIONAL LABOUR ORGANIZATION** (1990). *Surveys of Economically Active Population, Employment, Unemployment and Underemployment: An ILO Manual on Concepts and Methods*. Geneva.

▸ **INTERNATIONAL LABOUR ORGANIZATION** (2000). *Current International Recommendations on Labour Statistics, 2000 Edition*. Geneva.

▸ **INTERNATIONAL LABOUR ORGANIZATION** (2003). *Laborsta—an International Labour Office database on labour statistics operated by the ILO Bureau of Statistics*. Internet site http://laborsta.ilo.org . Geneva.

▸ **INTERNATIONAL LABOUR ORGANIZATION** (annual). *Key Indicators of the Labour Market*. Geneva. Available in part from http://www.ilo.org/kilm.

▸ **INTERNATIONAL LABOUR ORGANIZATION** (annual). *Yearbook of Labour Statistics*. Tables 3A-3E. Geneva. Available from http://laborsta.ilo.org.

▸ **ORGANISATION FOR ECONOMIC CO-OPERATION AND DEVELOPMENT** (2003). Standardized Unemployment rates for OECD countries. In *Main Economic Indicators*. Paris. Available from http://www.oecd.org. Select: Employment/ Statistics/Indicators.

▸ **UNITED NATIONS** (2003). *Millennium Indicators Database*. Statistics Division Internet site http://millenniumindicators.un.org.

▸ **UNITED NATIONS, AND INTERNATIONAL LABOUR ORGANIZATION BUREAU OF STATISTICS** (2002). *Collection of Economic Characteristics in Population Censuses*. Technical report. ST/ESA/STAT/119.

▸ **WORLD BANK** (2003 and annual). *World Development Indicators*. Print and CD-ROM. Washington, D.C. Available in part from http://www.worldbank.org/data.

AGENCIES
Ministries of labour
National statistical offices
International Labour Organization

46 PROPORTION OF POPULATION WITH ACCESS TO AFFORDABLE, ESSENTIAL DRUGS ON A SUSTAINABLE BASIS

DEFINITION

The *proportion of population with access to affordable essential drugs on a sustainable basis* is the percentage of the population that has access to a minimum of 20 most essential drugs. *Access* is defined as having drugs continuously available and affordable at public or private health facilities or drug outlets that are within one hour's walk of the population. *Essential drugs* are drugs that satisfy the health care needs of the majority of the population. The World Health Organization has developed the Model List of Essential Drugs, which is regularly updated through widespread consultations with member States and other partners. Progress in access to essential medicines is thus the result of combined effort by governments, strategic partners such as United Nations agencies, public-private partnerships, non-governmental organizations and professional associations (WHO Expert Committee on Essential Drugs, November 1999).

GOAL AND TARGET ADDRESSED

Goal 8. Develop a global partnership for development

Target 17. In cooperation with pharmaceutical companies, provide access to affordable, essential drugs in developing countries

RATIONALE

Millions of people die prematurely or suffer unnecessarily each year from diseases or conditions for which effective medicines or vaccines exist. Essential drugs save lives and improve health, but their potential can only be realized if they are accessible, rationally used and of good quality.

METHOD OF COMPUTATION

The World Health Organization regularly monitors access to a minimum of 20 most essential drugs.

DATA COLLECTION AND SOURCE

The Action Programme on Essential Drugs of the World Health Organization periodically interviews experts in each country about the pharmaceutical situation, asking them to rate access by the population to essential drugs at less than 50 per cent, 50–80 per cent, 80–95 per cent or more than 95 per cent (WHO Expert Committee on Essential Drugs, November 1999).

PERIODICITY OF MEASUREMENT

National data series are currently available for 1995 and 1997. Regional aggregates are currently available for 1987 and 1999.

REFERENCES AND INTERNATIONAL DATA COMPARISONS

▸ UNITED NATIONS (2003). *Millennium Indicators Database.* Statistics Division Internet site http://millenniumindicators.un.org.

▸ WORLD HEALTH ORGANIZATION (1997). *The WHO Model List of Essential Medicines- The 13th Model List of Essential Medicines.* Geneva. Available from http://www.who.int/medicines.

▸ WORLD HEALTH ORGANIZATION (1998). *Progress of WHO Member States in Developing National Drug Policies and in Revising Essential Drugs Lists.* WHO/DAP/98.7. Geneva. Available from http://www.who.int/medicines.

WHO produces country data series and regional aggregates.

AGENCIES

Ministries of health
World Health Organization

47 TELEPHONE LINES AND CELLULAR SUBSCRIBERS PER 100 POPULATION

DEFINITION

Telephone lines refer to the number of telephone lines connecting subscribers' terminal equipment to the public switched network and that have a dedicated port in the telephone exchange equipment.

Cellular subscribers refers to users of cellular telephones who subscribe to an automatic public mobile telephone service that provides access to the public switched telephone network using cellular technology.

GOAL AND TARGET ADDRESSED

Goal 8. Develop a global partnership for development

Target 18. In cooperation with the private sector, make available the benefits of new technologies, especially information and communications

RATIONALE

Indicator 47 and indicators 48A and B are important tools for monitoring progress towards Goal 8, because effective communication among those involved in the development process is not possible without the necessary infrastructure. Personal computers and telephones allow people to exchange experiences and learn from each other, enabling higher returns on investment and avoiding problems of duplication or missing information. The use of information and communication technologies can make Governments more transparent, thereby reducing corruption and leading to better governance. It can help people in rural areas find out about market prices and sell their products at a better price. It can also overcome traditional barriers to better education by making books available online and opening the door to e-learning.

METHOD OF COMPUTATION

Total telephone lines (see "DEFINITION") are divided by the population and multiplied by 100. Total cellular subscribers (see "DEFINITION") are divided by the population and multiplied by 100.

DATA COLLECTION AND SOURCE

Data on telephone lines and cellular subscribers are collected through annual questionnaires that the International Telecommunication Union (ITU) sends to government telecommunication agencies. The questionnaire is supplemented by annual reports of industry organizations to cross-check accuracy and to obtain data for countries that do not reply to the questionnaire.

PERIODICITY OF MEASUREMENT

Annual.

COMMENTS AND LIMITATIONS

Data for telephone lines come from administrative records compiled by national regulatory authorities or telecommunication operators and tend to be timely and complete. However, there are comparability issues for mobile subscribers owing to the prevalence of prepaid subscriptions. Those issues arise from differences in the time period chosen for determining when a prepaid subscription is considered no longer active.

REFERENCES AND INTERNATIONAL DATA COMPARISONS

▸ INTERNATIONAL TELECOMMUNICATION UNION (2003). World *Telecommunication Indicators Database*. Geneva. Available from http://www.itu.int/ITU–D/ict/publications/world/world.html.

▸ INTERNATIONAL TELECOMMUNICATION UNION (annual). *Yearbook of Statistics*. Geneva. Available from http://www.itu.int/ITU-D/ict.

▸ UNITED NATIONS (2003). *Millennium Indicators Database*. Statistics Division Internet site http://millenniumindicators.un.org.

AGENCY
International Telecommunication Union

PERSONAL COMPUTERS IN USE PER 100 POPULATION

DEFINITION
Personal computers (PCs) are computers designed to be operated by a single user at a time.

GOAL AND TARGET ADDRESSED
Goal 8. Develop a global partnership for development

Target 18. In cooperation with the private sector, make available the benefits of new technologies, especially information and communication technologies

RATIONALE
Indicators 47 and 48 are important tools for monitoring progress towards Goal 8, because effective communication among those involved in the development process is not possible without the necessary infrastructure. Personal computers and telephone lines allow people to exchange experiences and learn from each other, enabling higher returns on investment and avoiding problems of duplication or missing information. The use of information and communication technologies can make Governments more transparent, thereby reducing corruption and leading to better governance. It can help people in rural areas find out about market prices and sell their products at a better price. It can also overcome traditional barriers to better education by making books available online and opening the door to e-learning.

METHOD OF COMPUTATION
The total number of PCs in a country is divided by the population and multiplied by 100.

DATA COLLECTION AND SOURCE
Data are based largely on responses to a questionnaire that the International Telecommunication Union sends to government telecommunication agencies. In the absence of data from countries, the number of PCs is estimated using industry sales data or PC imports data.

DISAGGREGATION ISSUES
Data for PCs come from administrative and operational records that do not disaggregate the data.

PERIODICITY OF MEASUREMENT
Annual.

COMMENTS AND LIMITATIONS
Very few countries have a precise measure of the number of PCs. For some small developing economies, neither sales nor import data are available. PC data are quite recent, so long time series exist only for developed countries and major developing countries.

REFERENCES AND INTERNATIONAL DATA COMPARISONS

▶ INTERNATIONAL TELECOMMUNICATION UNION (2003). *World Telecommunication Indicators Database.* Geneva. Available from http://www.itu.int/ITU–D/ict/publications/world/world.html.

▶ INTERNATIONAL TELECOMMUNICATION UNION (annual). Yearbook of Statistics. Geneva. Available from http://www.itu.int/ITU-D/ict.

▶ UNITED NATIONS (2003). *Millennium Indicators Database.* Statistics Division Internet site http://millenniumindicators.un.org.

AGENCY
International Telecommunication Union

INTERNET USERS PER 100 POPULATION

DEFINITION
The *Internet* is a linked global network of computers in which users at one computer, if they have permission, get information from other computers in the network.

GOAL AND TARGET ADDRESSED

Goal 8. Develop a global partnership for development

Target 18. In cooperation with the private sector, make available the benefits of new technologies, especially information and communications

RATIONALE

Indicators 47 and 48 are important tools for monitoring progress towards Goal 8, because effective communication among those involved in the development process is not possible without the necessary infrastructure. Personal computers and telephone lines allow people to exchange experiences and learn from each other, enabling higher returns on investment and avoiding problems of duplication or missing information. The use of information and communication technologies can make Governments more transparent, thereby reducing corruption and leading to better governance. It can help people in rural areas find out about market prices and sell their products at a better price. It can also overcome traditional barriers to better education by making books available online and opening the door to e-learning.

METHOD OF COMPUTATION

The total number of Internet users is divided by the population and multiplied by 100.

DATA COLLECTION AND SOURCE

Internet user statistics are based largely on responses to an annual questionnaire that the International Telecommunication Union sends to government telecommunication agencies. For most developed and larger developing countries, Internet user data are based on methodologically sound user surveys conducted by national statistical agencies or industry associations. The data are either provided directly to the ITU by each country, or the ITU does the necessary research to obtain the data. For countries where Internet user surveys are not available, the ITU uses average multipliers to estimate the number of users per subscriber.

GENDER ISSUES

Surveys have been conducted by some countries providing a breakdown between male and female Internet users. The surveys indicate that more men than women use the Internet. Since the availability of gender-disaggregated statistics for this indicator is limited, however, little is known about use by gender.

DISAGGREGATION ISSUES

Internet user data can be disaggregated by gender, age, frequency of use, household income, location of access and other variables. However, this information is available only for a limited number of countries that collect data on information and communication technology use in household surveys.

PERIODICITY OF MEASUREMENT

Annual.

COMMENTS AND LIMITATIONS

The quality of Internet user data varies, and the quality of data for smaller developing countries is uncertain. The data can also be misleading owing to multiple prepaid Internet accounts, free Internet access accounts or public Internet access such as Internet cafés.

REFERENCES AND INTERNATIONAL DATA COMPARISONS

- INTERNATIONAL TELECOMMUNICATION UNION (2003). *World Telecommunication Indicators Database*. Geneva. Available from http://www.itu.int/ITU-D/ict/publications/ world/world.html.
- INTERNATIONAL TELECOMMUNICATION UNION (annual). *Yearbook of Statistics*. Geneva. Available from http://www.itu.int/ITU-D/ict.
- UNITED NATIONS (2003). *Millennium Indicators Database*. Statistics Division Internet site http://millenniumindicators.un.org.

AGENCY

International Telecommunication Union

ANNEX 1

Additional socio-economic common country assessment indicators

 PROPORTION OF CHILDREN UNDER AGE 15 WHO ARE WORKING

DEFINITION

Proportion of children under age 15 who are working refers to children who are employed in an economic activity for pay, profit or family gain. *Economic activity* covers the production of goods and services for pay or profit or for use by own household. *Employed* means being engaged in an economic activity during a specified reference period or being temporarily absent from such an activity.

GOAL AND TARGET ADDRESSED

Goal. Reduce child labour

Target. Elimination of child labour (World Summit on Sustainable Development, 1995)

RATIONALE

The indicator monitors the degree to which the youth labour force is utilized in the economy and therefore serves as a measure of the success of strategies to create jobs for youth.

METHOD OF COMPUTATION

The number of children who are employed is divided by the number of children of the same age group in the population.

DATA COLLECTION AND SOURCES

Data come from population censuses, labour force surveys, special child labour surveys, Multiple Indicator Cluster Surveys (http://www.childinfo.org), Demographic and Health Surveys (http://www.measuredhs.com), Living Standards Measurement Study surveys (http://www.worldbank.org/lsms) and Core Welfare Indicators Questionnaires (http://www4.worldbank.org/afr/stats/cwiq.cfm).

PERIODICITY OF MEASUREMENT

Results from population censuses are normally available every 10 years. Labour force surveys may be available annually or more frequently in developed countries, but are generally available every three to five years in developing countries. The other surveys are produced only occasionally.

GENDER ISSUES

The available data indicate that boys are more likely to be economically active than girls. Girls are more often engaged in household services.

COMMENTS AND LIMITATIONS

Reliable estimates of child labour are difficult to obtain. In many countries child labour is assumed not to exist and therefore is excluded from official statistics. Some estimates cover only children ages 10–14. Others cover children ages 5–14. Still others cover different age ranges.

Not all work is harmful to a child's development. The International Labour Organization has addressed this concern, for example, by differentiating acceptable work from unacceptable labour. The United Nations Children's Fund sometimes also distinguishes between different types of work and different ages of children.

REFERENCES AND INTERNATIONAL DATA COMPARISONS

▶ HUSSMANNS, R., F. MEHRAN AND V. VERMA (1990). *Surveys of Economically Active Population, Employment, Unemployment and Underemployment: An ILO Manual on Concepts and Methods*. Geneva.

▶ INTERNATIONAL LABOUR ORGANIZATION (2000). *Current International Recommendations on Labour Statistics, 2000 Edition*. Geneva.

▶ INTERNATIONAL LABOUR ORGANIZATION (2002). *Every Child Counts: New Global Estimates on Child Labour*. Geneva.

▶ INTERNATIONAL LABOUR ORGANIZATION (2003). *International Programme on the Elimination of Child Labour: IPEC*. Geneva. Internet site http://www.ilo.org/public/english/standards/ipec/.

▸ **INTERNATIONAL LABOUR ORGANIZATION** (annual). *Yearbook of Labour Statistics*. Geneva. Available from http://laborsta.ilo.org.

▸ **UNITED NATIONS CHILDREN'S FUND** (2003). *Progress since the World Summit for Children*. New York. Available from http://www.childinfo.org. Select: Quick Access/Child labour.

▸ **UNITED NATIONS, AND INTERNATIONAL LABOUR ORGANIZATION** (2002). *Collection of Economic Characteristics in Population Censuses*. Technical Report. ST/ESA/STAT/119.

▸ **WORLD BANK** (2003 and annual). *World Development Indicators*. Print and CD-ROM. Notes to table 2.3. Washington, DC. Available in part from http://www.worldbank.org/data.

AGENCIES

International Labour Organization
United Nation's Children's Fund

CCA 30 EMPLOYMENT TO POPULATION OF WORKING AGE RATIO

DEFINITION

Population of working age covers people ages 15–64. *Employment* is defined according to international definitions and refers to being engaged in an economic activity during a specified reference period, or being temporarily absent from such an activity. *Economic activity* covers all production of goods and services for pay or profit or for use by own household.

Working age is usually determined on the basis of national circumstances, such as the age at which most children have completed compulsory education and the age at which any general old age pension system can be claimed. The United Nations recommends that population census tabulations on the employed distinguish those 15 years and older from those younger than 15 years old.

GOAL AND TARGET ADDRESSED

Goal. Creation of full employment
Target. Universal access to paid employment (World Summit on Sustainable Development, 1995)

METHOD OF COMPUTATION

The number of people who are employed is divided by the total number of people in the selected age interval for working age, generally 15–64.

DATA COLLECTION AND SOURCE

Data are collected through population censuses, labour force surveys and official national estimates.

PERIODICITY OF MEASUREMENT

Results from population censuses are normally available every 10 years. Labour force surveys may be available annually or more frequently in developed countries, but are generally available every three to five years in developing countries. The other surveys are produced occasionally.

GENDER ISSUES

Male employment rates are generally higher than female employment rates. Female employment rates are often underestimated because many economic activities in which women dominate are not recorded as employment. This may influence the international comparability of employment rates.

COMMENTS AND LIMITATIONS

Measuring employment is more straightforward where labour markets are well developed and a large proportion of the population gains its livelihood from a market economy.

REFERENCES AND INTERNATIONAL DATA COMPARISONS

▸ **HUSSMANNS, R., F. MEHRAN** and **V. VERMA** (1990). *Surveys of Economically Active Population, Employment, Unemployment* *and Underemployment: An ILO Manual on Concepts and Methods*. Geneva.

- ▸ INTERNATIONAL LABOUR ORGANIZATION (2000). *Current International Recommendations on Labour Statistics*, 2000 Edition. Geneva.
- ▸ INTERNATIONAL LABOUR ORGANIZATION (annual). *Yearbook of Labour Statistics*. Geneva. Available from http://laborsta.ilo.org.
- ▸ UNITED NATIONS (2003). *Methods and Classifications*. Statistics Division Internet site http://unstats.un.org/unsd/methods.htm .
- ▸ UNITED NATIONS, AND INTERNATIONAL LABOUR ORGANIZATION (2002). *Collection of Economic Characteristics in Population Censuses* Technical Report. ST/ESA/STAT/ 119.
- ▸ WORLD BANK (2003 and annual). *World Development Indicators*. Print and CD-ROM. Notes to table 2.3 and 2.4. Washington, DC. Available in part from http://www.world-bank.org/data.

AGENCY
International Labour Organization

 UNEMPLOYMENT RATE

DEFINITION
Unemployment covers all people who, during a specified reference period, are not employed, are available for work and have taken concrete steps to seek paid employment or self-employment during a recent period. *The labour force* consists of those who are employed plus those who are unemployed during the relevant reference period. *Employed* means being engaged in an economic activity during a specified reference period or being temporarily absent from such an activity. *Economic activity* refers to all production of goods and services for pay or profit or for use by own household.

GOAL AND TARGET ADDRESSED
Goal. Creation of full employment
Target. Universal access to paid employment (World Summit on Sustainable Development 1995)

METHOD OF COMPUTATION
The number of people who are unemployed is divided by the number of people in the labour force.

DATA COLLECTION AND SOURCE
Data are collected from population censuses, labour force surveys, Demographic and Health Surveys (http://www.measuredhs.com), Living Standards Measurement Study surveys (http://www.worldbank.org/lsms) and Core Welfare Indicators Questionnaires (http://www4.worldbank.org/afr/stats/cwiq.cfm).

PERIODICITY OF MEASUREMENT
Results from population censuses are normally available every 10 years. Labour force surveys may be available annually or more frequently in developed countries, but are generally available every three to five years in developing countries. The other surveys are produced only occasionally.

GENDER ISSUES
Female unemployment rates are often significantly higher than male unemployment rates.

COMMENTS AND LIMITATIONS
The concepts of *employment* and *unemployment* have different relevance depending on the level of labour market development and the presence of a market economy. People living in regions of a country where there is little or no formal employment would not usually be classified as "unemployed" even if they are without work and would accept a job if offered one (discouraged workers). Unemployment estimates can also understate problems in labour markets when people are discouraged from seeking work because jobs are scarce or nonexistent.

Only household surveys can give reliable estimates according to the international definition. Employment services and unemployment compensation schemes that are well developed (such as those in OECD countries) can derive reliable unemployment estimates from records of unemployment registration or from national insurance records.

REFERENCES AND INTERNATIONAL DATA COMPARISONS

▸ HUSSMANNS, R., F. MEHRAN and V. VERMA (1990). *Surveys of Economically Active Population, Employment, Unemployment and Underemployment: An ILO Manual on Concepts and Methods*. Geneva.

▸ INTERNATIONAL LABOUR ORGANIZATION (2000). *Current International Recommendations on Labour Statistics, 2000 Edition*. Geneva.

▸ INTERNATIONAL LABOUR ORGANIZATION (annual). *Yearbook of Labour Statistics*. Geneva. available from http://laborsta.ilo.org.

▸ UNITED NATIONS, and INTERNATIONAL LABOUR ORGANIZATION (2002). *Collection of Economic Characteristics in Population Censuses*. Technical Report. ST/ESA/STAT/119.

▸ WORLD BANK (2003 and annual). *World Development Indicators*. Print and CD-ROM. Notes to 2.5. Washington, DC. Available in part from http://www.worldbank.org/data.

AGENCY
International Labour Organization

 INFORMAL SECTOR EMPLOYMENT AS A PERCENTAGE OF EMPLOYMENT

DEFINITION
Informal sector employment includes all people who, during a given reference period, were employed in at least one informal sector enterprise, irrespective of their status in employment (employer, own-account worker, contributing family worker, employee or member of a producers cooperative) or whether it was their main or second job.

Informal sector enterprises are defined by the following criteria: they are household unincorporated enterprises (excluding quasi-corpo-

rations) as defined by the System of National Accounts 1993; they produce at least some of their goods or services for sale or barter; they are engaged in non-agricultural activities (including secondary non-agricultural activities of enterprises in the agricultural sector); and their size (in number of employees) is below a specified threshold, determined according to national circumstances, or they are not registered under specific forms of national legislation (such as commercial acts, tax or social security laws, professional groups, regulatory acts, or similar acts, laws or regulations established by national legislative bodies), or none of their employees is registered. Households producing domestic or personal services in employing paid domestic employees may be included.

Employed means being engaged in an economic activity during a specified reference period or being temporarily absent from such an activity. *Economic activity* refers to all production of goods and services for pay or profit or for use by own household

GOAL AND TARGET ADDRESSED
Goal. Creation of full employment
Target. Universal access to paid employment (World Summit on Sustainable Development, 1995)

METHOD OF COMPUTATION
The number of people classified as employed in the informal sector in their main or second jobs is divided by the total number of people employed in the same geographical areas, branches of economic activity, age group or other defining characteristic.

DATA COLLECTION AND SOURCES
Data are collected through informal sector surveys, Labour force surveys and Multiple Indicator Cluster Surveys.

PERIODICITY OF MEASUREMENT
Informal sector surveys are generally carried

out ad hoc, often with intervals of five or more years. Labour force surveys tend to be conducted more frequently, generally every three to five years in developing countries.

GENDER ISSUES
There are large gender-specific differences in informal sector employment in most countries.

INTERNATIONAL DATA COMPARISONS
Major limitations on the international comparability of data result from the inclusion or exclusion of agricultural activities from the scope of the informal sector, the inclusion or exclusion of informal sector activities undertaken as second jobs, differences in the geographical coverage of informal sector surveys and similar factors.

COMMENTS AND LIMITATIONS
Statistics on employment in the informal sector tend to be available only for developing countries and transition countries, where the informal sector plays a significant role in employment and income generation. Informal employment outside informal sector enterprises is not covered by the enterprise-based definition of the informal sector. Although there are international standards, definitions may vary among countries.

REFERENCES AND INTERNATIONAL DATA COMPARISONS
▶ INTERNATIONAL LABOUR OFFICE (2002). *Women and Men in the Informal Economy: A statistical picture*. Geneva. available from http://www.ilo.org/public/english/employment/gems/download/women.pdf.
▶ INTERNATIONAL LABOUR ORGANIZATION (annual). *Key Indicators of the Labour Market*. Table 7. Geneva. Available in part from http://www.ilo.org/kilm.
▶ INTERNATIONAL LABOUR ORGANIZATION (2000). *Current International Recommendations on Labour Statistics*, 2000 Edition. Geneva.

AGENCY
International Labour Organization

CCA 41 NUMBER OF PERSONS PER ROOM, OR AVERAGE FLOOR AREA PER PERSON

DEFINITION
Number of persons per room, or average floor area per person, is a measure of crowding. *Number of persons per room* is the number of rooms in the living quarters of a household per person in the household. *Average floor area* (in square metres) *per person* is the median usable floor area per person.

The *number of rooms* excludes kitchens, bathrooms, toilets, verandas, rooms used for business and rooms let to tenants.

Floor area includes kitchens, bathrooms, internal corridors and closets. Covered, semi-private spaces such as corridors, inner courtyards or verandas are included in the floor area if they are used for cooking, eating, sleeping or other domestic activities.

GOAL AND TARGET ADDRESSED
Goal. Adequate shelter for all
Target. Provision of sufficient living space and avoidance of overcrowding (United Nations Conference on Human Settlements, [Habitat II], 1996)

RATIONALE
Crowding, or housing density, is a key measure of housing quality. The three most commonly used measures of crowding are persons per room, floor area per person and households per dwelling unit. Surveys have shown that floor area per person is the more precise and more policy sensitive of the three.

METHOD OF COMPUTATION
The number of persons per room is calculated by dividing the number of people who live in the household by the total number of rooms

they occupy. A low indicator denotes low crowding (density).

The area per person is calculated by dividing the floor area in square metres by the number of people in the household. A low indicator denotes high crowding (density).

DATA COLLECTION AND SOURCE
The data are mainly collected from population censuses and from household surveys such as Living Standards Measurement Study surveys (http://www.worldbank.org/lsms), Multiple Indicator Cluster Surveys (http://www.childinfo.org), Demographic and Health Surveys (http://www.measuredhs.com) and Core Welfare Indicators Questionnaires (http://www4.worldbank.org/afr/stats/cwiq.cfm).

GENDER ISSUES
In many countries, households headed by women are more crowded than those headed by men.

PERIODICITY OF MEASUREMENT
Population censuses are every 10 years or less. Household surveys are generally conducted every three to five years.

COMMENTS AND LIMITATIONS
Data on the two indicators were collected during the first phase of the joint UN–HABITAT–World Bank Housing Indicators Programme (1992). Results vary considerably when collected in different areas: urban, rural and national. Informal settlements and disadvantaged groups tend to have less space. Housing size and housing quality are not always linked, for economic and cultural reasons. Floor area is preferred for accuracy and sensitivity to policy, but some censuses and surveys collect only number of rooms.

REFERENCES AND INTERNATIONAL DATA COMPARISONS
▸ **UNITED NATIONS** (2001). *Compendium of Human Settlements Statistics*. Sales No.

E.01.XVII.5.
▸ **UNITED NATIONS** (2001). *Indicators of Sustainable Development: Guidelines and Methodologies*. Sales No. E.01.II.A.6. Available from http://www.un.org/esa/susdev/natlinfo/indicators/isd.htm.
▸ **UNITED NATIONS HUMAN SETTLEMENTS PROGRAMME (UN-HABITAT)** (1995). *Human Settlement Interventions: Addressing Crowding and Health Issues*. (HS/374/95/E). Nairobi.
▸ **UNITED NATIONS HUMAN SETTLEMENTS PROGRAMME (UN-HABITAT)** (2003). *Global Urban Observatory*. Internet site http://www.unhabitat.org/programmes/guo. Nairobi.
▸ **UNITED NATIONS HUMAN SETTLEMENTS PROGRAMME (UN-HABITAT)** (2003). Internet site http://www.unhabitat.org and http://www.unhabitat.org/mdg. Nairobi.
▸ **WORLD BANK** (2003 and annual). *World Development Indicators*. Print and CD-ROM. Notes to table 3.11. Washington, DC. Available in part from http://www.worldbank.org/data .

AGENCY
United Nations Human Settlements Programme

 **NUMBER OF INTENTIONAL HOMICIDES PER 100,000 INHABITANTS**

DEFINITION
Homicide is defined by the United Nations Interregional Crime and Justice Research Institute as the killing of any human being by the act, procurement or omission of another. (The term *murder* is usually applied to unlawful and premeditated homicide.)

GOAL AND TARGET ADDRESSED
Goal. Improve crime prevention
Target. Eliminate/significantly reduce violence and crime (United Nations Congress on the Prevention of Crime and Treatment of Offenders, 1995)

METHOD OF COMPUTATION
The indicator is calculated as the ratio of number of the intentional homicides to the total population multiplied by 100,000.

DATA COLLECTION AND SOURCE
Crime data, including homicide data, are derived mainly from the administration records of criminal justice ministries. Population data come from censuses.

GENDER ISSUES
Women commit fewer crimes than men generally, including homicide. Women are also less often the victims of homicide.

PERIODICITY OF MEASUREMENT
Administrative data on crimes are normally available annually. Census data are usually collected every 10 years.

COMMENTS AND LIMITATIONS
Since crime data are dependent on national definitions and reporting procedures, they are often not comparable internationally.

More comparable and more consistent data are derived from household crime victim surveys, but such surveys are not universal and are often taken only in capital cities.

REFERENCES AND INTERNATIONAL DATA COMPARISONS
▸ UNITED NATIONS CRIME AND JUSTICE INFORMATION NETWORK(UNCJIN) (2003). Internet site http://www.uncjin.org. Vienna.
▸ UNITED NATIONS OFFICE ON DRUGS AND CRIME (2003). Internet site http://www.odccp.org/odccp/crime_cicp_sitemap.html. Vienna.

AGENCIES
United Nations Office on Drugs and Crime
United Nations Interregional Crime and Justice Research Institute

ANNEX 2
Household surveys and other national data sources

Annex 2 reviews Multiple Indicator Cluster Surveys, Demographic and Health Surveys, Living Standards Measurement Studies, Core Welfare Indicators Questionnaires in Africa, household budget surveys, labour force surveys, household surveys with an institutional component, censuses of population and housing, other surveys and administrative data.

All household surveys and censuses provide data by gender and age and by many other classifying variables. TABLE A2 at the end of the present annex shows the topics covered by the Multiple Indicator Cluster Surveys, Demographic and Health Surveys, Living Standards Measurement Studies and Core Welfare Indicators Questionnaires in Africa.

MULTIPLE INDICATOR CLUSTER SURVEY
To provide recent data for assessing progress towards the 1990 World Summit for Children goals, the United Nation's Children's Fund developed the Multiple Indicator Cluster Surveys (MICS) in 1994 to obtain data on a small subset of the goals. Experience from this work was used in developing a revised and expanded Survey (known as MICS2) for assessing progress at end-decade. The surveys were conducted in 66 countries during 1999–2001, primarily by national government ministries with support from a variety of partners.

The main subjects of MICS2 are health and education; TABLE A2 shows which indicators are likely to be included. MICS2 is modular and so the surveys may not be identical. More information can be found at http://www.childinfo.org.

DEMOGRAPHIC AND HEALTH SURVEY
Demographic and Health Surveys (DHS) are sponsored by the United States Agency for International Development and undertaken by Macro International, Inc. They were first conducted in 1984 as successors to the International Statistical Institute World Fertility Surveys. The Demographic Health Surveys are now in their fourth series. The abbreviated name was changed in 1997 to DHS+. They have been undertaken in over 60 countries. Some countries have had only one DHS, but others have had several. Most surveys are addressed to about 5,000 households.

Most questions refer to demography and to health including nutrition, but they also include other topics, such as education. TABLE A2 shows the indicators likely to be covered by the DHS. More information can be found at www.measuredhs.com.

LIVING STANDARDS MEASUREMENT STUDY
The first Living Standards Measurement Study (LSMS) surveys were launched by the World Bank in Côte d'Ivoire and Peru in 1985. Since then there have been about 40 surveys in 25 countries. They have been sponsored by various donors, including the World Bank and the United States Agency for International Development, and by some countries.

Although the first few LSMS surveys followed a similar format, they have varied considerably since then. There are standard LSMS modules, but they are often omitted. The organization of the fieldwork also varies. Most are one-off sample surveys, but a four-wave panel was also undertaken in the Kagera region of Tanzania.

TABLE A2 shows the indicators likely to be covered by LSMS. More information can be found at http://www.worldbank.org/lsms.

CORE WELFARE INDICATORS QUESTIONNAIRE SURVEY IN AFRICA

The Core Welfare Indicators Questionnaire (CWIQ) survey is relatively new. Developed by the World Bank, it was piloted in Kenya in 1996 and in Ghana in 1997. The questionnaires are relatively short (about eight sides), but other modules may be added. The surveys are intended to be annual and to have samples of 5,000 to 15,000 households. The questionnaire is designed to complement other surveys as part of a national monitoring package. It is intended to contribute to statistical capacity-building in developing countries. The results are intended to be available within a few weeks of data collection.

TABLE A2 shows the indicators likely to be covered by the CWIQ. More information can be found at http://www4.worldbank.org/afr/stats/cwiq.cfm.

HOUSEHOLD BUDGET SURVEYS

Household budget surveys (HBS) are intended for various purposes, including measurement of poverty and of household consumption of goods and services for weighting consumer prices. Their value as sources of other data derive from the inclusion of a variety of questions among basic or general variables. This offers the possibility of cross-classifying them against many other variables, including income and urban or rural location as well as all the common classifiers such as age and gender.

The surveys are complex and expensive, so they are not conducted very frequently in developing countries. They are undertaken often enough (perhaps every five years or so) in many countries to provide fairly up-to-date and fairly frequent data, however.

The Income Consumption and Expenditure Survey (ICES) in Zimbabwe is an example of a household budget survey. The 2001 survey is the most recent, and the ICES has been con-

ducted there approximately every five years since 1985.

LABOUR FORCE SURVEYS

Labour force surveys (LFS) have become widespread in industrialized countries, but are more rare in developing countries. They are intended to provide information on employment and unemployment, but they also frequently seek information on education and training and may include other variables. They occasionally include questions on income from employment. For reasons of efficiency, they generally cover the non-institutional population. In developing countries, they are often undertaken only in urban areas

SURVEYS WITH AN INSTITUTIONAL COMPONENT

Some household surveys are also accompanied by surveys addressed to local institutions, including schools and hospitals. The Zimbabwe Sentinel Surveillance Survey, for example, includes institutional components addressed to schools and to health establishments. Thus they are able to provide data on facilities serving households.

CENSUSES OF POPULATION AND HOUSING

A population census is the primary source of information about the number of people in a country and the characteristics of the population. Several features distinguish a census from survey-based sources of data. It can achieve complete coverage of the population. It offers possibilities for relating individual characteristics of the population with those of households. It provides details about subnational population groups. Owing to its high cost, it has the disadvantage of being able to provide data only once every 10 years, or sometimes less, and the questionnaires have to be relatively short.

The census is the unique basic source of benchmark demographic data, such as number of people by age and gender. Demographic data are used as denominators for ratios of all kinds, on school enrolment for example, and for many other common country assessment and Millennium Development Goals indicators. However, population estimates have to be updated between censuses, and national methods and standards can differ. Many international agencies use United Nations estimates of population as denominators for ratios in order to be consistent between countries. Nevertheless, the United Nations population estimates, which are revised every two years, are often different from the national estimates, mainly (but not always) as a result of international standardization.

Censuses are also sometimes used as sampling frames for sample surveys.

REFERENCES :

▶ UNITED NATIONS. (1998). *Principles and Recommendations for Population and Housing Censuses, Revision 1*. Series M, No. 67. Sales No. E.98.XVII.1.

▶ UNITED NATIONS POPULATION FUND (2002). *Population and Housing Censuses: Strategies for Reducing Costs*. Available from: http://www.unfpa.org/upload/lib_pub_ file/24_filename_pophousingcensus.pdf.

▶ UNITED NATIONS POPULATION FUND (2003). *Counting the People: Constraining Census Costs and Assessing Alternative Approaches*. Available from: http://www.unfpa.org/ upload/ lib_pub_file/184_filename_popdev-strat-7.pdf.

OTHER SURVEYS

There are also many household surveys of variable frequency, or ad hoc, that are either general in their purpose or have a limited range of purposes. There are special surveys on particular topics, such as some limited aspect of health.

Survey programmes pertinent to the data for common country assessment and Millennium Development Goals indicators, in addition to those mentioned above, include the following:
- HIV/AIDS, various epidemiological surveys

(Joint United Nations Programme on HIV/AIDS)
- Tuberculosis/DOTS (notification programme); Roll Back Malaria (World Health Organization)
- Pilot surveys in selected countries to test/improve methodologies of data collection on labour force (International Labour Organization)
- Child labour survey (International Labour Organization)
- Informal sector surveys (International Labour Organization)
- Pilot surveys in selected countries to test/improve methodologies of data collection on nutrition (Food and Agriculture Organization of the United Nations)
- Pilot small-scale studies on education/literacy (United Nations Educational, Scientific and Cultural Organization)
- Access to personal computers and the Internet (International Telecommunication Union)
- Secure tenure and slum improvement (United Nations Human Settlements Programme)

ADMINISTRATIVE SOURCES

The most commonly used sources of data for education, and often for health, are administrative sources—data derived from the administration of education or health. Unemployment data are also frequently derived from administrative registrations of employment offices. The data are made available by ministries and sometimes by national statistical offices. Data on births and deaths are also frequently drawn from administrative sources, usually vital statistics registration systems.

Administrative sources can potentially provide data for very small areas. Their disadvantages include bias, application of national standards and definitions, and non-response. For vital statistics, such as births and deaths, and for many other indicators, the data often do not exist or are incomplete.

GOALS	LSMS	DHS	CWIQ	MICS[a]
GOAL 1: ERADICATE EXTREME POVERTY AND HUNGER				
Proportion of population below $1 per day[b]	•[c]			
Poverty gap ratio [incidence x depth of poverty]	•			
Share of poorest quintile in national consumption	•			
Prevalence of underweight children under 5 years of age	•	•	•	•
Proportion of population below minimum level of dietary energy consumption[d]				
GOAL 2: ACHIEVE UNIVERSAL PRIMARY EDUCATION				
Net enrolment ratio in primary education[e]	(•)	(•)	(•)	(•)
Proportion of pupils starting grade 1 who reach grade 5	•	•	•	•
Literacy rate of 15–24 year-olds	•	•	•	•
GOAL 3: PROMOTE GENDER EQUALITY AND EMPOWER WOMEN				
Ratio of girls to boys in primary, secondary and tertiary education[f]	(•)	(•)	(•)	(•)
Ratio of literate women to men, 15–24 years old				
Share of women in wage employment in the non-agricultural sector	•	•	•	•
Proportion of seats held by women in national parliament	•			
GOAL 4: REDUCE CHILD MORTALITY				
Under-five mortality rate		•		•
Infant mortality rate		•		•
Proportion of 1-year-old children immunized against measles		•		•
GOAL 5: IMPROVE MATERNAL HEALTH				
Maternal mortality ratio		•		•
Proportion of births attended by skilled health personnel		•		•
GOAL 6: COMBAT HIV/AIDS, MALARIA AND OTHER DISEASES				
HIV prevalence among aged pregnant women 15–24 years				
Contraceptive prevalence rate[g]		•		•
Number of children orphaned by HIV/AIDS				
Prevalence and death rates associated with malaria				•[i]
Proportion of population in malaria-risk areas using effective malaria prevention and treatment measures[h]				
Prevalence and death rates associated with tuberculosis				
Proportion of tuberculosis cases detected and cured under DOTS				
GOAL 7: ENSURE ENVIRONMENTAL SUSTAINABILITY				
Proportion of land area covered by forest				
Ratio of area protected to maintain biological diversity to surface area				
Energy use (kg oil equivalent) per $1 GDP (PPP)				
Carbon dioxide emissions per capita and consumption of ozone-depleting CFCs (ODP tons)				
Proportion of population using solid fuels				
Proportion of population with sustainable access to an improved water source, urban and rural[j]	•	•	•	•
Proportion of urban and rural population with access to improved sanitation	•	•	•	•
Proportion of households with access to secure tenure	(•)[k]			

TABLE A2 (CONTINUED)

NOTES

a. The Multiple Indicator Cluster Survey (MICS) is made up of modules, and not all modules were used in all countries. This column is based on the full questionnaire using all modules.

b. For monitoring country poverty trends, indicators based on national poverty lines should be used, where available.

c. This indicator also requires the calculation of a national PPP, which in turn is derived from internationally coordinated price collection conducted by the International Comparison Programme.

d. National data are provided by the Food and Agriculture Organization of the United Nations based on a statistical modeling technique.

e. All surveys collect school attendance, rather than enrolment. However, it could be argued that this has greater policy relevance at the national level. Enrolment rates in international reporting are based on administrative records.

f. The ratio is of attendance rates, not enrolment rates.

g. Among contraceptive methods, only condoms are effective in preventing HIV transmission. The contraceptive prevalence rate is also useful in tracking progress in other health, gender and poverty goals. Since the condom use rate is measured only among women in union, it is supplemented by an indicator on condom use in high-risk situations (indicator 19A) and an indicator on HIV/AIDS knowledge (indicator 19B).

h. Prevention can be measured by the percentage of children under five sleeping under insecticide-treated bednets. Treatment can be measured by the percentage of children under five who are appropriately treated.

i. For children under five only.

j. All surveys measure access to improved source, but do not assess whether it is sustainable.

k. Surveys typically ask about type of dwelling and tenure. They may not explicitly address the issue of how secure is, for example, a rental agreement, but that could be covered in the future.

ANNEX 3
Web sites
(see also references in the metadata sheets)

▸ United Nations. Millennium Development Goals. http://www.un.org/millenniumgoals

▸ United Nations Statistics Division. Millennium Indicators Database. http://millenniumindicators.un.org

▸ United Nations Statistics Division. http://unstats.un.org/unsd

▸ World Bank. Millennium Development Goals. http://www.developmentgoals.org

▸ Organisation for Economic Co-operation and Development. http://www.oecd.org/dac. Under Topics, select: Aid statistics, Aid effectiveness and donor practices or Millennium Develement Goals

▸ Core Welfare Indicators Questionnaire (CWIQ) surveys. Available from http://www4.worldbank.org/afr/stats/cwiq.cfm

▸ Demographic and Health Surveys. http://www.measuredhs.com

▸ Food and Agriculture Organization of the United Nations. http://www.fao.org

▸ International Labour Organization. http://www.ilo.org/stat

▸ World Health Organization/United Nations Environment Programme Intergovernmental Panel on Climate Change. http://www.ipcc.ch

▸ IUCN–World Conservation Union. http://www.iucn.org

▸ Living Standards Measurement Study (LSMS). http://www.worldbank.org/lsms

▸ Multiple Indicator Cluster Surveys (MICS). Available from http://www.childinfo.org

▸ Organisation for Economic Co-operation and Development. Development Assistance Committee. http://www.oecd.org/dac

▸ United Nations Development Group. http://www.undg.org

▸ United Nations Development Programme. Human Development Report. Available from http://www.undp.org/hdr2003

▸ United Nations Environment Programme. http://www.unep.org

▸ UNEP. Land use. Available from http://www.unep.org/themes/land

▸ United Nations Educational, Scientific and Cultural Organization. http://www.unesco.org

▸ UNESCO Institute for Statistics. http://www.uis.unesco.org

▸ United Nations Children's Fund. http://www.unicef.org and http://www.childinfo.org

▸ United Nations Framework Convention on Climate Change. http://unfccc.int

▸ United Nations Population Fund. http://www.unfpa.org

▸ United Nations Human Settlements Programme. http://www.unhabitat.org and http://www.unhabitat.org/campaigns/tenure/introduction.asp

▸ Cities in a Globalizing World. Available from http://www.earthscan.co.uk/cities

▸ United Nations Interregional Crime and Justice Research Institute. http://www.unicri.it

▸ World Conservation Monitoring Centre. Protected area data unit. http://www.wcmc.org.uk/data

▸ Joint United Nations Programme on HIV/AIDS. http://www.unaids.org/hivaidsinfo

▸ World Health Organization. Directly observed treatment short course (for tuberculosis). Available from http://www.who.int/gtb/dots

▸ Stop TB Partnership. http://www.stoptb.org

▸ World Bank. http://www.worldbank.org/data

▸ World Bank. World Development Indicators. Available from http://www.worldbank.org/data

▸ World Resources Institute. http://www.earthtrends.wri.org

▸ Biosphere reserves. http://www.unesco.org/mab

▸ Heritage sites. http://www.unesco.org/whc

▸ Wetlands. http://www.ramsar.org/sitelist.pdf

ANNEX 4
World summits and conferences

International Conference on Primary Health Care, Almaty, Kazakhstan, 1978

World Conference to Review and Appraise Achievements of the United Nations Decade for Women: Equality, Development and Peace, Nairobi, 1985

World Conference on Education for All, Jomtien, Thailand, 1990

World Summit for Children, New York, 1990

International Conference on Nutrition, Rome, 1992

United Nations Conference on Environment and Development, Rio de Janeiro, Brazil, 1992

World Conference on Human Rights, Vienna, 1993

Global Conference on the Sustainable Development of Small Island Developing States, Bridgetown, 1994

International Conference on Population and Development, Cairo, 1994

Fourth World Conference on Women, Beijing, 1995

Ninth United Nations Congress on the Prevention of Crime and the Treatment of Offenders, Cairo, 1995

World Summit for Social Development, Copenhagen, 1995

United Nations Conference on Human Settlements (Habitat II), Istanbul, 1996

World Food Summit, Rome, 1996

World Conference of Ministers Responsible for Youth, Lisbon, 1998

Twentieth special session of the General Assembly on the world drug problem, New York, 1998

Global Conference on the Sustainable Development of Small Island Developing States, New York, 1999

Tenth United Nations Congress on the Prevention of Crime and the Treatment of Offenders, Vienna, 2000

World Education Forum, Dakar, 2000

Twenty-fourth special session of the General Assembly: World Summit for Social Development and beyond: achieving social development for all in a globalizing word, Geneva, 2000

World Summit on Sustainable Development, Johannesburg, South Africa, 2002